To Mary, Mike, Lucy, Sophie, Alexandra and Jonathan,

Wishing you all a very
HAPPY CHRISTMAS!.
and thank-you for all your
help making our wedding
so special.

With much love from,
Jane and Rémy

Christmas 1992

PHILIP'S

PARIS

ARCHITECTURE · HISTORY · ART

PHILIP'S

PARIS

ARCHITECTURE · HISTORY · ART

IAN LITTLEWOOD

PHOTOGRAPHY BY JOHN HESELTINE

GEORGE
PHILIP

The pictures on the following pages are reproduced by kind permission of Giraudon/Bridgeman Art Library: 46, 52, 81, 95, 96, 137, 150, 167, 173

TITLE PAGE *The basilica of Sacre-Coeur rising above the skyline of Montmartre to the north.*

First published by George Philip Limited, 59 Grosvenor Street, London W1X 9DA

Text © Ian Littlewood 1992
Photographs © John Heseltine 1992
Maps © George Philip Limited 1992
Appendices © George Philip 1992

British Library Cataloguing in Publication Data

Littlewood, Ian
    Paris: architecture, history, art.
    I. Title
    914.43604838

ISBN 0540012548

Page design by Gwyn Lewis
Maps by Lois J. Wright
Typeset by Tradespools Limited
Printed in Hong Kong

Contents

....

Preface

....

It is one of the virtues of Paris that it can be seen on foot. In spite of its variety of monuments scattered in different locations, there are few of the exhausting route marches that are the tourist's usual penance in a capital city. In London anything, even the underground, is better than having to walk half-way across the city centre, but a walk, say, from the Opéra to the Jardin du Luxembourg or from the place Saint-Michel to the Eiffel Tower is among the keenest pleasures that Paris has to offer.

This propaganda for walking is not entirely disinterested. Each of the chapters that follow is presented in the form of a walk. To set them out in this way is largely a matter of convention – it would be a resolute tourist who actually followed the routes step by step – but I would like to think that parts of them, at least, will tempt readers out of their armchairs and on to the pavements. The itineraries make no claim to be comprehensive. I have taken the reader to the places I like and pointed to the aspects of them that appeal to me, trying on the way to convey something of their individual flavour.

For the purposes of this book the city has been divided into seven sections, beginning where Paris itself began, on the Île de la Cité, and moving round in an anticlockwise spiral chapter by chapter. This makes the whole business sound rather neater than in fact it is; there are detours, excursions, backtrackings and, no doubt, occasional perversities, but I hope the reader will find that in the end most of the city has been covered in one chapter or another. If a favourite church has been missed or a gallery slighted, I can only apologize and again hope that elsewhere I have redeemed the fault by drawing your attention to an unfamiliar park or a previously unvisited museum. How much of it all you choose to sample will of course depend on your preferences. There are regular visitors to Paris who never set foot inside a gallery or museum, others who go there for little else. In any case, for those who grow weary of sight-seeing there is always that quintessential Parisian distraction, the pavement café, where half an afternoon can slip

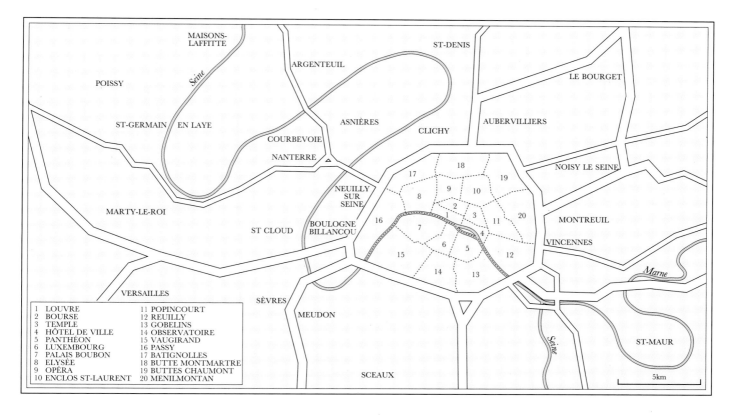

PARIS AND ITS ENVIRONS

1	LOUVRE	11	POPINCOURT
2	BOURSE	12	REUILLY
3	TEMPLE	13	GOBELINS
4	HÔTEL DE VILLE	14	OBSERVATOIRE
5	PANTHÉON	15	VAUGIRARD
6	LUXEMBOURG	16	PASSY
7	PALAIS BOUBON	17	BATIGNOLLES
8	ELYSÉE	18	BUTTE MONTMARTRE
9	OPÉRA	19	BUTTES CHAUMONT
10	ENCLOS ST-LAURENT	20	MENILMONTAN

by in a pleasant mist of white wine and well-being while the world goes on around you. And since you are in Paris and on holiday, why not? After all, the Louvre will still be there tomorrow.

Introduction

....

Paris's appeal lies in its potent combination of sex, art, fashion and food. Confined to their damp islands, the British have for centuries looked longingly across the Channel towards a city where all these valuable commodities are taken seriously, where they are matters of connoisseurship and debate, to be approached with enjoyment and a certain daring. To most Americans, until World War I, it was all rather remote, but then they too came under the spell of Paris. When the Volstead Act of 1919 introduced Prohibition throughout the country, it added another spur to those who felt the lure of less moralistic climes. Paris meant liberation; it represented the cosmopolitan rather than the provincial, the free-thinking rather than the bigoted, the experimental rather than the cautious. Over the years it has been a city of *salons* and brothels and boulevards and cafés, of *haute couture* and *haute cuisine*, of intellectual passion and romantic love and artistic adventure, of all the refinements of civilized life. There are cities one escapes to and cities one escapes from. Among the former, Paris is pre-eminent.

My own entanglement with the place began 25 years ago. One summer evening, I was dropped on the outskirts of Paris by a friendly Volkswagen that had given me a lift from somewhere in the south. I spent the night wandering around the streets of the unfamiliar city. I had no map, so it was pure chance that brought me to the pont des Arts just as the sky was beginning to show the first signs of light. I sat there watching the day break beyond Notre-Dame, completely intoxicated by the sight, and it seemed for the moment as though all the myths that I had ever encountered about Paris might be confirmed in reality. I have been going back ever since.

I did not know it at the time, but the island in front of me as I looked out from the pont des Arts was the place where Paris had been born. It must have looked an inhospitable spot to the ragged tribe of Parisii who came here in the third century BC. At first they scarcely knew what to make of it. Part of the tribe forged on and eventually found their way across the Channel and up to Yorkshire, the

OPPOSITE *The late nineteenth-century pont Alexandre III seen from the Right Bank with the contrasting landmarks of the Tour Montparnasse and the Église du Dôme of the Invalides in the background.*

other part stayed on. It was a raw and marshy resting-place, this cluster of islands in the middle of the Seine; but it commanded the river crossings, and that meant power. The Parisii flourished. By the time of Julius Caesar they were a force to be reckoned with, and they paid the penalty. Crushed by Caesar's lieutenant Labienus in 52 BC, they saw what was left of their town occupied by the Roman troops. It was called Lutetia at the time, and this was the beginning of its history.

Rebuilt by the Romans, Lutetia enjoyed a modest role as an increasingly prosperous city on the fringes of the empire. Spread out across the slopes of the Mont Sainte-Geneviève on the left bank, it was equipped with the usual trappings of a provincial Roman town, including a forum, an amphitheatre and the baths which survive in fragmentary form today. This was the first of the periodic phases of building that have shaped the city. The barbarian invasions of the late third century forced the boundaries back to the fortified area of the Cité, where Julian the Apostate was later proclaimed Roman Emperor in 361. Thereafter, his 'beloved Lutetia', which at about this time became Paris, developed little until the massive building programme of King Philippe-Auguste at the end of the twelfth century. It was he who created the first substantial wall around the city and went on to protect it with the original fortress of the Louvre. Over the next couple of centuries the left bank, occupied primarily by the university and the abbey of Saint-Germain-des-Prés, remained much the same size, while the right bank expanded towards the new line of fortifications set up by Charles V, with the Bastille guarding the eastern approach. In the sixteenth century these defences were somewhat extended, producing a northern boundary to the city more or less along the line of the inner circle of boulevards. It was not until just before the Revolution that Paris acquired something like its modern dimensions with the construction of the huge Farmers General Wall. Punctuated by 57 toll houses, this enclosed the whole city along what is now the line of the outer boulevards. The wall was less a military fortification than a commercial one, designed to facilitate the collection of customs duties from those entering the city. The farmers general after whom the wall is named were responsible for staffing the customs posts. They paid a sum annually to the royal treasury based on the anticipated revenue and pocketed the difference, which was usually substantial. The wall was, therefore, met with murmurs of disfavour by the local population, hence the common saying: *'Le mur murant Paris rend Paris murmurant'*.

As the city grew, so different figures made their various contributions to its shape. We can thank Henri IV for the place des Vosges (the place Royale, as it was then) and therefore indirectly for the consequent development of the surrounding area of the Marais. The first half of the seventeenth century, dominated by Richelieu, saw the beginnings of the Faubourg Saint-Germain and also the start of work on the Île Saint-Louis, two areas that were to become centres of aristocratic life and that have survived largely intact to the present day. Both Louis XIV and Louis XV shared a taste for grandiose building projects, and the century and a half leading up to the Revolution produced many of the landmarks that are still familiar. The *grands boulevards*, the Invalides, the Palais Bourbon, the

OPPOSITE *From the place Louis-Lépine, the Sainte Chapelle rises above the buildings of the Palais de Justice.*

The pont des Arts and the tower of Notre-Dame looking towards the western tip of the Île de la Cité.

Val-de-Grâce, the place de la Concorde and the Panthéon all belong to this period. In the nineteenth century, under Napoleon III, the overpowering influence was that of Baron Haussmann. The emperor had made him prefect of the Seine in 1853 and gave him licence to improve the city. He demolished whole areas of Paris, replacing the cramped – and politically dangerous – streets of the old city with the avenues and boulevards that we walk through today. Since then the skyline has changed from time to time as various different leaders have sought to leave their mark on the capital, but the basic outlines of central Paris have remained much the same for over a century now.

This book is an exploration of Paris rather than of Paris's history, but to make sense of the city at least a smattering of history is essential. After the various wars, feuds and divisions of the kingdom that marked the first millenium of her existence, Paris emerged as the centre of a country that was growing in power as it gradually became more united. But then, in the middle of the twelfth century, the seeds were sown of the fatal hostility that was to set France against England for a good part of the next 700 years. After the annulment of her marriage to Louis VII, Eleanor of Aquitaine swiftly married Henry Plantagenet, later Henry II of

England. This marriage gave the English king legal claim to a large chunk of France and so became the basis of a series of conflicts that reached a long climax in the Hundred Years War.

Paris, meanwhile, was torn by conflicts of its own. In the early fifteenth century Charles VI, a near-imbecile misguidedly dubbed '*le Bien-Aimé*', had sparked a violent revolt among the citizens by his excessive taxation. Before long his power had effectively been surrendered to the rival factions of the Armagnacs and the Burgundians. With the support of the Burgundians Henry V of England invaded France and won a crushing victory at Agincourt. Although Joan of Arc failed to regain Paris and was finally captured by the Burgundians and burned at the stake in Rouen in 1431, her example inspired continued resistance to the English occupying forces. With the exception of Calais, the occupation was finally brought to an end in the middle of the fifteenth century. Life for the average Parisian during these years was grim indeed. Cold, hunger and disease were not the only perils. 'The sixteenth day of December,' noted the anonymous author of the *Journal d'un bourgeois de Paris* in 1439, 'wolves came suddenly and devoured four housewives, and the following Friday they struck panic into seventeen of them around the city, of whom eleven died from their injuries.'

A period of relative stability followed, broken by footling wars in Italy. Then in the second half of the sixteenth century the country was plunged into religious turmoil – partly thanks to the bigoted influence of Catherine de' Medici, whose handiwork can be seen in the Massacre of St Bartholomew on 23 August 1572. Not without reason, the French in general and Parisians in particular revere the monarch who put a stop to this carnage. Henri of Navarre was a man without religious prejudice. A Protestant who had fought against the Catholics, he cheerfully switched his religion (supposedly remarking '*Paris vaut bien une messe*') in order to gain entrance to Paris and recognition as King Henri IV. By the Edict of Nantes he then ensured that Protestants who took a less flexible view of their religion would not be persecuted for adhering to it.

He had not been long dead before France was at war again. And so it went on, through the reigns of Louis XIII, Louis XIV and Louis XV: the Thirty Years War, the civil war of the Fronde, the war against the Dutch, the war against the Grand Alliance, the war of the Spanish Succession (celebrated in England for the victories of Marlborough), the war of the Polish Succession, the war of the Austrian Succession, the Seven Years War – most of them wars of personal or national aggrandisement, most of them ruinously expensive. To the other troubles of the economy, which included the outrageous cost of building Versailles, Louis XIV added in 1685 the revocation of the Edict of Nantes. The effect of this was to drive many Huguenots out of the country and seriously undermine the industries that relied on them.

As the economy plunged further towards crisis, France under Louis XVI was drawn stage by stage into the vortex of the Revolution. The figure who emerges from these years of Revolution, towering over the destiny of France, is of course Napoleon Bonaparte. After his exile to St Helena in 1815, the restoration of the

Bourbon dynasty produced a couple of undistinguished kings, in the shape of Louis XVIII and Charles X, before the July revolution of 1830 put an end to the Bourbons for good. What followed was scarcely more impressive. Louis-Philippe, the favoured candidate of the *haute bourgeoisie*, was overthrown by another revolution in 1848, to be succeeded some time later by Bonaparte's nephew, the unappealing Louis-Napoléon. As Napoleon III he presided over the Second Empire, dragging France into yet more wars which culminated in her total defeat by the Prussians in 1870 and the emperor's exile to England.

During the twentieth century, it is again the periods of conflict which loom largest in France's history, although neither of the World Wars caused extensive damage to the capital. In recent years, the city has suffered more from the efforts of ambitious statesmen, greedy speculators and visionary architects than from any external enemy. This long chronicle of war and revolution is balanced by a cultural history of unsurpassed splendour, which has always been focused on one city. An overwhelming number of the people who wanted to paint pictures, write plays, compose music, design buildings or promote ideas came here. The city became more than the French capital, it became the capital of all things French.

The dangerous Paris of the fifteenth century that saw the horrors of the Hundred Years War also witnessed the career of France's greatest medieval poet, François Villon. If the sixteenth century was racked by petty wars with Italy and religious strife, it was also the century that produced under the patronage of François I the art of Jean and François Clouet and the paintings of the École de Fontainebleau. It was the century in which Rabelais created his satirical giants Gargantua and Pantagruel, Michel de Montaigne wrote his essays and the poets of the Pléiade, among them Ronsard, Jodelle and du Bellay, set out to transform the nature of French verse. The catalogue of civil war, military folly, political and religious oppression that marks the reigns of the Bourbon monarchs from Louis XIII to Louis XVI is counterpointed by the catalogue of artistic and intellectual achievement of the same period. The buildings of Mansart, Libéral-Bruant and Le Vau, the gardens of André le Nôtre, the music of Couperin and Rameau, the letters of Mme de Sévigné, the writings of Voltaire and Rousseau, the creation of the *Encyclopédie* by Diderot and d'Alembert, all these belong to the Paris of the seventeenth and eighteenth centuries, as does that most Parisian institution, the *salon*. From her famous *chambre bleue*, so called because its walls were hung with blue, Mme de Rambouillet deliberately set out to civilize the manners and conversation of seventeenth-century Paris. With the aid of figures like Voiture, La Rochefoucauld and Mlle de Scudéry, she exercised a crucial influence over the society of her day. The tradition was continued in the eighteenth century by such hostesses as Mme du Deffand and Mme Geoffrin, who drew to their *salons* a dazzling mixture of courtiers, poets, politicians and philosophers. While they talked, France slipped towards revolution; some of their ideas helped it on its way. To see the disparities that were a catalyst to revolution, we need only turn from the scenes of desperate poverty in working-class Paris to the exquisite furniture that was one of the triumphant achievements of the reigns of Louis XV and XVI.

Auguste Rodin's Ugolin et ses Enfants *in the grounds of the Hôtel Biron, the museum holding many of his most famous works.*

The atmosphere of Paris under Louis-Philippe and Napoleon III could scarcely have seemed more inimical to culture. It was the era of the bourgeois and the philistine. And yet long after the philistines have been forgotten, the works of Hugo, Balzac, Flaubert, Baudelaire, Rimbaud, Zola and Mallarmé will be remembered. With the birth of Impressionism in the 1870s Paris became the focus of new developments in western art. The early years of the twentieth century saw a succession of artistic movements which originated or took root here. Fauvism, Cubism, Futurism, Surrealism were all in one way or another indebted to the restless intellectual energy that seems to permeate the air Parisians breathe. Perhaps it is partly the tradition of café life, stretching back to the eighteenth century and beyond, that has made the city such a crucible for ideas. Certainly, there is a veneration for the intellect and a delight in abstract thought which were as much a part of the Paris of the existentialists in the 1940s and 1950s or the Structuralists and post-Structuralists in the 1960s and 1970s as they were of the Paris that produced the *encyclopédistes* in the eighteenth century.

All this has understandably fuelled the nation's pride in its capital city. The results have been mixed. On the one hand, its status as a showcase for the grandeur of its monarchs and political leaders has produced some notable acts of vandalism, but on the other, this national pride in the city has inspired a persistent concern to make and keep it beautiful. What happens to London excites resentment, sometimes even controversy, but on the whole there is little sense that national self-esteem is bound up with the appearance and amenities of the capital. In Paris, the reverse is true and the tourist benefits.

For the French, eating is a matter of importance. Experienced visitors will have their favourite restaurants, others will rely on chance, intuition and their guidebook. I would merely remind you of the gourmet's pleasures that can be found outside the restaurant – in the *pâtisserie* and the *charcuterie* and the ravishing displays of the market stall. All of them demand lengthy and detailed investigation. On the subject of money, it is perhaps worth repeating that there are very few cities in the world where it is a good idea to change money in one's hotel. In Paris the banks are the safest option. There are occasional bureaux de change where you can get better rates, but these have to be looked for; they are greatly outnumbered by the ones that apparently offer higher rates but then deduct a staggering percentage for their commission.

In general, life is not difficult for the tourist in Paris. With its boulevards, parks and pavement cafés it is a city that lends itself to pleasure. Over the years much of it has been changed, much destroyed, but many of the districts preserve an individual character of their own. The seventeenth-century streets of the Marais, the old hôtels of the Faubourg Saint-Germain, the noisy, youthful atmosphere of Saint-Michel, the seedy nightlife around Pigalle, the tranquil byways that are still to be found in Montmartre – all of them make their distinctive contribution to the experience of Paris. It is part of the extraordinary charm of this city that within a narrow compass it offers a compendium of urban pleasures. Among the beautiful old streets of Saint-Germain-des-Prés, for example, surrounded by art galleries, antique shops and restaurants, you are side by side with the fashionable excitements of the boulevard and only a stone's throw from romantic promenades along the banks of the Seine. A stroll across the pont des Arts and you are at the entrance of the Louvre, to your left the elegant gardens of the Tuileries, to your right the dubious delights of the rue Saint-Denis. We are back where we started: sex, art, fashion and food.

OPPOSITE *Caught in the sunlight, the gilded dome of the Invalides stands out from the Paris rooftops.*

1
The Islands and
Les Halles

....

NOTRE-DAME *to* SAINT-GERMAIN-L'AUXERROIS

Notre-Dame is probably the one cathedral in Europe that even the most casual tourist can bring to mind without hesitation. Among jumbled memories of gothic spires, arching vaults and acres of gargoyle-encrusted stone, its twin towers stand out with unmistakable clarity. For 700 years they have dominated the Île de la Cité, and today they still rise with splendid confidence above the undistinguished lumber of official architecture that occupies much of the rest of the island. What sort of impression must this great church have made when around its base there was nothing but a clutter of wooden hovels?

Directly in front of the main entrance, about twenty-five metres away, a small star has been set into the pavement to mark the centre of Paris. This is the *Point Zéro*, the spot in relation to which all distances to and from the city are measured. It is a point of departure in more ways than one, for this is where Paris itself began – as you can see if you walk to the back of the square, where a sign indicates the entrance to the archaeological crypt. It was during excavations carried out in 1965 that the remains now displayed here came to light. What we see is a cross-section of the history of this part of Paris, and there is no better place to start a tour of the city. It is a curious experience to leave the crowds of tourists milling around in front of the cathedral and descend into this quiet underworld, where one finds oneself looking at the vestiges of medieval hospitals, of streets and houses long disappeared, of ramparts that were thrown up at a time when the Roman Empire was still the most powerful force on earth. The crypt is carefully lit and its exhibits well explained. Running through the centre is what remains of the rue Neuve-Notre-Dame, the original street laid out in the thirteenth century to lead to the cathedral. As one stands beside it in this darkened chamber, the past seems very close.

The siting of Notre-Dame just here was not a matter of chance; it had been a place of worship for thousands of years. The earliest cults are lost in prehistory,

OPPOSITE *St Stephen's portal and the south-east transept of Notre-Dame. Restored in the mid nineteenth century, Notre-Dame is one of the most spectacular medieval cathedrals in Europe.*

19

THE ÎLE DE LA CITÉ, THE ÎLE SAINT-LOUIS AND LES HALLES

but a few metres from the *Point Zéro* another plaque marks the spot where the sixth-century church of St-Étienne stood from Merovingian times until it was demolished to make way for the new cathedral.

NOTRE-DAME was begun in the middle of the twelfth century at the instigation of the energetic Maurice of Sully, Bishop of Paris, and took the better part of 200 years to complete. Though clearly gothic in appearance, it still owes much to the Norman Romanesque. There is an appealing simplicity about the basic design of the main west façade, rising in three tiers which get steadily lighter as they ascend. At the focal point, the Virgin and Child are represented in the centre of the rose window, which acts as a sort of halo around them.

All three of the west portals feature aspects of the Virgin. The details, though much restored, make a fascinating study. Among the oldest statues are those in

The tympanum of the thirteenth-century cloister portal of Notre-Dame, showing in the upper register scenes from a mystery play performed on the parvis, and below scenes from the life of the Virgin.

the right-hand portal, above the scenes of the nativity, which show Mary with Bishop Maurice standing on her right and King Louis VII kneeling on her left. (The significance of this distinction would not have been lost on either party.) Other dignitaries of the church fare less well. If you look at the horrible tangle of devils at the bottom of the archivolts on the right of the central portal, you can see the unusual sight of a female devil urinating with evident satisfaction on the head of a mitred bishop.

Apart from the portals in the west façade, St Stephen's portal in the south and the cloister portal in the north are both superb examples of thirteenth-century art. St Stephen's is railed off now, making it difficult to see the details, but on the pier of the cloister portal stands a beautiful figure of the Virgin, whose child was removed during the Revolution. Notice also the depiction of the

Massacre of the Innocents in which two vividly carved soldiers in chain mail, looking as though they have come straight from the retinue of William the Conqueror, carry out the murder.

Like most churches in Paris, Notre-Dame has had a chequered history. While it was still under construction, it provided a temporary home for the Crown of Thorns; during the Revolution it did the same for 1500 casks of wine. This was an undignified but welcome alternative to demolition. Its main role during this turbulent period was as a Temple of Reason. To celebrate the transformation a ballet dancer was enthroned on the high altar and the statues of the saints were replaced by statues of Voltaire and Rousseau. Later, Napoleon made Notre-Dame the scene of his coronation. All went well until the moment when the pope was supposed to put the crown on the emperor's head, at which point the thought of having a partner in his moment of glory proved too much for Napoleon; he snatched away the crown and did the job himself.

For the next few decades the church went into a decline. After the hardships of the Revolution it was sadly in need of restoration; instead, it suffered an extended period of neglect. The decorations crumbled, the stonework decayed, cracks began to open in the fabric. Popular indifference was rapidly effecting the destruction it had escaped during the Revolution. At this point, Victor Hugo came on the scene. His novel *Notre-Dame de Paris*, published in 1831, did much to restore the church's fortunes. In this story of the beautiful gypsy girl and the hunchbacked bell-ringer, Hugo clothed the somewhat battered old structure with all the glamour of romance, and in doing so he argued powerfully that the present state of the church was a national disgrace. The mood of the time was in his favour. Under the supervision of Eugène-Emmanuel Viollet-le-Duc, the work of restoration went on through the middle years of the century. It had not been long finished when the revolutionaries of the Commune burst in on Good Friday 1871 and the church was again on the edge of destruction. In the event, the attempt to put it to the torch was foiled by the medical students of the neighbouring Hôtel Dieu.

Having survived the Communards, as earlier it had survived the zealots of the Revolution, Notre-Dame has now to survive the tourists. And so does anyone who wants to look at the interior. Whatever the time of year, you are likely to find yourself in a crowd of fellow-visitors – weighed down by the morning's shopping, grappling with new rolls of film, struggling in pursuit of elusive tour leaders. When it was built, Notre-Dame could accommodate something like ten per cent of the city's whole population, which was then around a hundred thousand. Today it needs all its space and more. Fortunately, the jam of sightseers affects only the ground level; the church is rescued by its height. As one looks upwards, the human presence dwindles. However great the crowds, one's impression on entering Notre-Dame is still of space and height.

The gallery along either side cuts down the amount of light in the church, but this is to some extent offset by the two magnificent rose windows in the transepts, which have a diameter of almost 43 feet. Comparing them, you might sense that

OPPOSITE *Christ surrounded by saints and angels in the rose window of the south transept of Notre-Dame.*

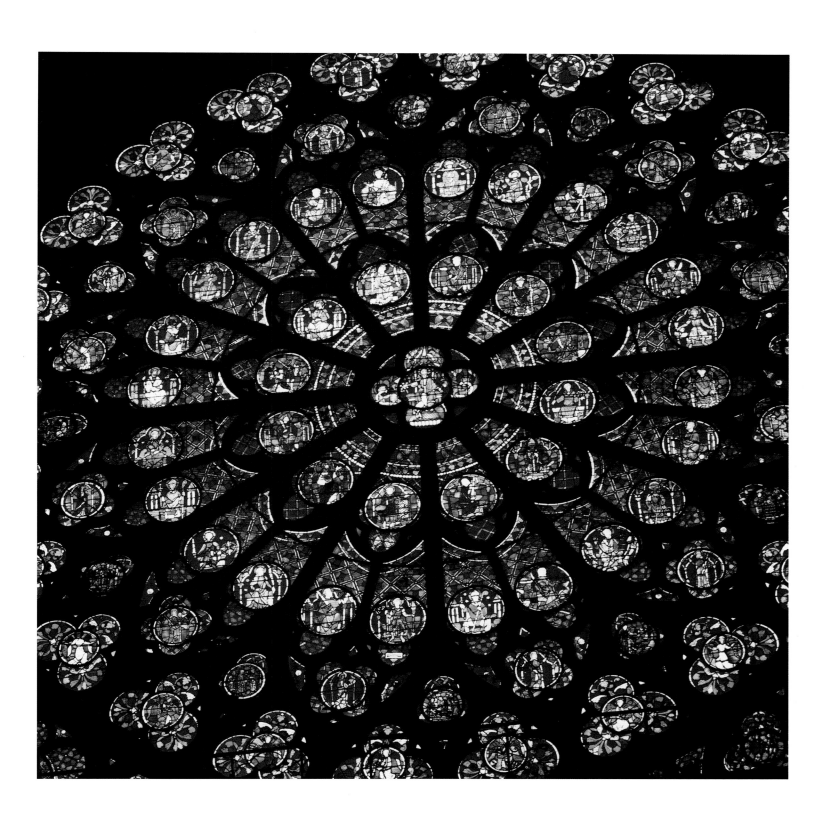

the north window is somehow lighter, less solid than its companion. This is not just a question of colour and structure. Look closely and you will see that none of the radial spokes of the north window are precisely aligned with either the vertical or the horizontal axis. The same was originally true of the south window, but in replacing it Viollet-Le-Duc straightened its axis and thereby perhaps took away a fraction of its life.

The square, or *parvis*, in front of the church was much enlarged in the nineteenth century. Although we can now move back far enough to get a full view of the façade, the dominating scale of the cathedral has been sadly reduced. From the Middle Ages through to the eighteenth century a small scaffold was periodically erected on the *parvis* at the foot of which condemned criminals, carrying a yellow wax candle, came to make the so-called *amende honorable*. With bare feet and bare head, dressed in a shift and with a rope around their neck, they publicly confessed their sins and begged for absolution. A placard pinned to their chest and back specified the crime for which they were to be executed. From here it was only a short step to the bloody entertainments of the place de Grève, where they met their end.

The question now is whether or not you have the stamina for an ascent of the towers. If the answer is yes, then you must go round the north side of the church and enter from the rue du Cloître-Notre-Dame. In the interests of safety the top of the south tower has been completely wired over, so one walks round in a sort of cage, which rather diminishes the pleasure of the unaccustomed views along the Seine. There are in all some 238 steps to the top of the tower, quite enough to make many prefer to go round the other way and wait in the relatively peaceful square Jean XXIII. As you walk along beside the river, note the spectacular flying buttresses as well as Viollet-le-Duc's nineteenth-century spire. It is one of the distinctive features of Notre-Dame that it looks beautiful not only from the front and sides, but also from the back. Sitting under the trees, alongside the idling tour buses, we can get a final perspective on the majestic achievement of this church.

Across the road is the small patch of ground called the square de l'Île-de-France, where two narrow flights of steps lead down to a sombre memorial to the 200,000 French men and women deported to Nazi concentration camps and killed there during World War II. It is a moving and imaginative monument. Inside the main enclosure a tunnel leads off, flanked by a long panel on either side, inset with tokens numbering the dead. This melancholy place is comparatively little visited by the hordes who troop round nearby Notre-Dame.

From the top of the steps, we can look across to the stately houses of the Île Saint-Louis. In 1908 E.V. Lucas described the buildings as dull and dirty. Tastes have changed; when we see this lovely island today, it is hard to imagine that he was writing about the same place. Preserved from the more intrusive aspects of urban life, it breathes an atmosphere of moneyed seclusion. It is where the millionaire keeps his *pied-à-terre* and the minister of state goes home in the evening. Until the seventeenth century there were two islands here, which had been left more or less untouched. Within 50 years the Île Saint-Louis that we see now

OPPOSITE *One of Notre-Dame's gargoyles looks gloomily out across the city.*

came into being. And the startling thing is that what we see now really is the place that was created in the seventeenth century.

Crossing the bridge, we can turn to the right along the quai d'Orléans. Half way down the quay we reach the rue le Regrattier, whose name commemorates one of the men who put up the money for the development of the island. This is a charming spot, particularly on a summer afternoon, when the sun strikes through the deep covering of the poplar trees and glints off the Seine. From the angle of the quay one can look back towards the prow of Notre-Dame, and on the right to the lone eminence of the Tour Saint-Jacques rising above the surrounding roofs.

The house at 2, rue le Regrattier was the home in the 1920s of Nancy Cunard, the flamboyant upper-class rebel who founded the Hours Press in Paris. Among those she entertained here were George Moore, Louis Aragon and Tristan Tzara. A few doors further down, at number 6, is the house which Baudelaire furnished in oriental style for his 'Vénus noire', the mulatto actress Jeanne Duval. It was probably in 1843 that he met her, while he was living nearby in the Hôtel de Lauzun. Captivated by her huge eyes and feline grace, he installed her here and embarked on a relationship which, however disastrous it may have been personally, provided the inspiration for some of his greatest poetry.

Beside the end of the quai d'Orléans we pass the pont de la Tournelle, which since 1928, when it was last rebuilt, has been disfigured by Landowski's grotesque statue of St Geneviève, a futuristic production that would clearly be more at home on a launch pad in Florida. At the tip of the island – badly mauled in the 1870s by the construction of the pont de Sully – is the Hôtel Lambert. Standing just on the corner of the rue Saint-Louis-en-l'Île, it was the home in the eighteenth century of Mme du Châtelet. For a short time in the summer of 1742 she and Voltaire lived here during the course of their long liaison, which ended six years later when she replaced the philosopher with a young army officer.

Until the twentieth century the fashion was to avoid the sun rather than to seek it, and this northern side of the island was the more highly valued. Along the quai d'Anjou the most striking building, both architecturally and historically, is the Hôtel de Lauzun at number 17, built in the mid 1650s and recognizable at once by the dormer windows, the gilded central balcony and the engaging drainpipes which expand into fish below the first floor windows before returning to a more conventional shape.

The man for whom this mansion is named only lived here for a short while from 1682 to 1685, but he was one of the island's more colourful inhabitants. The Comte de Lauzun was not born to greatness; he had made his way in the court of Louis XIV by a mixture of wit, courage and bare-faced effrontery. On one occasion he had actually hidden under Mme de Montespan's bed to witness an assignation between her and the king. His fortunes changed when he became the object of the affections of the Duchesse de Montpensier, la Grande Mademoiselle. Six years older than Lauzun and a great deal bigger, she was also the king's cousin, which made her an extremely dangerous prize. Lauzun prevaricated as best he could, but the formidable Mademoiselle was hopelessly in love. She petitioned Louis to allow them to marry. After initially consenting, the king changed his mind and by way of insurance dispatched Lauzun to prison. There he remained for just over ten years while Mademoiselle pined for him and intrigued to secure his release. Whether or not there was ever a secret marriage, the relationship when Lauzun returned from prison in 1681 lurched from one crisis of recrimination to another. His lavish house on the quai d'Anjou was merely the scene of pleasures that fuelled her jealousy. It was a sad story that ended sadly, leaving the Grande Mademoiselle to drift towards a lonely old age.

Her lover, who lived on into his eighties in rude health, took the opportunity in 1685 to remove himself temporarily to the court of James II in England. On his departure the Hôtel de Lauzun was sold to the great-nephew of Cardinal Richelieu and his young wife, a convent girl of notably scandalous character. Saint-Simon describes her as '*belle comme le jour*', in spite of the fact that her front teeth had been taken out on the orders of her father to discourage the attentions of gallants. The couple quickly ruined themselves by high living, after which the hôtel passed into a succession of steadier hands until the 1840s when it numbered among its tenants both Charles Baudelaire and Théophile Gautier. It was during this period that it became the meeting-place of the 'Club des Haschichins', a group of bohemians who met to sample the delights of hashish in a congenially decadent atmosphere.

Just beyond the Hôtel de Lauzun, the rue Poulletier, whose name commemorates another of the island's developers, leads away from the quay to the late seventeenth-century church of SAINT-LOUIS-EN-L'ÎLE. This is not one of my favourite churches, partly because it contains some of the least attractive stained glass in Paris. More hideous even than the bright crucifixion above the main altar is the window in the south aisle depicting the devotion of France to the Sacred Heart. Presented by a senator and his family, it must have left the unfortunate vicar groping for appropriate words of thanks. Around the central scene a ring of cherubim bob above the clouds with wings that look like colourful life-jackets keeping them afloat on a stormy sea.

The church lost its main relic of St Louis during World War I but luckily had a piece of rib in reserve. As it happens, relics of St Louis are in plentiful supply. In order to get his remains back from Carthage, near where he died, the body was cut up and then boiled to separate the flesh from the bones. The less durable remains were shipped to the church of Monreale near Palermo, while the bones were finally brought back to Paris and in the course of the fourteenth century dispersed to various communities and churches that had an interest in the saint.

Most of the statues in the church went the usual way of ecclesiastical sculpture during the Revolution, but the Virgin and St Geneviève managed to escape destruction by posing for the duration as Reason and Liberty. Against a wall of the arch next to St Geneviève is a small plaque from the town of St Louis, Missouri, in memory of the saint in whose honour the American town was named.

From the church we can wander back to the quays to complete our circuit of the island, or continue up the rue Saint-Louis-en-l'Île past a string of pleasant

A drainpipe with a charming touch of fantasy from the Hôtel de Lauzun on the Île Saint-Louis.

The spire of the church of Saint-Louis-en-l'Île rises above the road named after it. Apart from the addition of shops at ground-floor level, many of the buildings on the island remain much as they were built.

and reasonably priced restaurants. Either way, if this is summer as one likes to imagine it, we shall want to stop at 31, rue Saint-Louis-en-l'Île, where, after waiting in the inevitable queue, we can visit Berthillon's to select from a range of ices that might include such delicacies as wild strawberries, mandarin, or *nougat au miel*.

After recrossing the pont Saint-Louis, we can turn to the right along the quai aux Fleurs, where a plaque between the doors of numbers 9 and 11 indicates the site of the house in which Abélard once lived. It was actually the home of a certain Canon Fulbert who lived here in the early years of the twelfth century. He must have thought he had done well to secure the brilliant young Pierre Abélard as a tutor for his niece. An opponent of the old scholasticism typified by his adversary Bernard of Clairvaux, Abélard was renowned both for his intellect and for his continence. The latter, at least, was a fiction. He had singled out Héloïse well in advance and offered Fulbert deliberately favourable terms to ensure that he could gain access to her. He was, by his own account, irresistible, and Héloïse seems anyway to have had little mind to resist. 'Our speech was more of love than of the books that lay open before us,' wrote Abélard; 'our kisses far outnumbered our reasoned words.' The result was a son, charmingly, if somewhat puzzlingly, named Astrolabe. Shortly afterwards the lovers married in secret and in another world might have lived happily ever after, or as happily as one could expect to live with anyone as objectionable as Abélard sounds from his autobiography. But Fulbert was a vengeful man. His henchmen came to Abélard by night and castrated him, and Héloïse was condemned to the life of a nun.

This is one area that can give us some idea of what the Île de la Cité must have looked like before most of the old streets were swept away in the middle of the nineteenth century. The flight of steps beside number 11 leads us down to the rue des Ursins. This, the rue des Chantres and the rue de la Colombe all preserve something of the atmosphere of earlier times. On the corner of the rue des Ursins and the rue de la Colombe are the remains, off limits to the public, of the little CHAPELLE DE SAINT-AIGNAN. Apart from Sainte Chapelle, this is the only survivor of some 23 medieval chapels and churches that were once scattered around the island. (You can see a fair number of them if you look at the model of the area in the Musée Carnavalet (pp. 148–51).) At about the time that Héloïse and Abélard were turning from books to lovers' vows, Bernard of Clairvaux was a regular preacher at this chapel, where he bewailed 'the dissolute life of those students who preferred to hear the jingle of the gilded buckles and belts of slenderwaisted harlots than the psalms of holy men'.

Just beyond the pont d'Arcole rises the forbidding structure of the HÔTEL DIEU. Built in the nineteenth century, this replaced the old Hôtel Dieu which stood on the other side of the island, more or less where the statue of Charlemagne is today. For well over 1000 years the Hôtel Dieu has been the city's main hospital. In the Middle Ages its beds were crammed with patients, sometimes as many as eight under one cover. Not infrequently the living found themselves sharing a bed with men who had already died but had simply not been removed. Hospital was very much a last resort. At the begining of the eighteenth century there were still 4000 men in the Hôtel Dieu, but in other respects things had perhaps looked up. The place was staffed by Augustinian nuns who, according to one contemporary traveller, 'look after the sick with so much tenderness sometimes, that they don't care much to return to the nunneries.' Not long before, he adds, 'a certain Irishman, being recovered by the care of his pretty nurse, made shift to carry her away without being ever heard of since.'

At the far end of the Hôtel Dieu we pass the pont Notre-Dame. Already sight and smell are drawing us beyond the bridge to the place Louis-Lépine, where a riot of plants and flowers spill out on to the pavement. Nearby is an attractive example of the old Métro stations – Cité – complete with orange lamps under the art nouveau cobra hoods at either side of the entrance. The Louis Lépine after whom the square is named was the man who introduced policemen's whistles and the distinctive white truncheons to Paris. He may not be a figure one would immediately associate with the flower market, but he seems well suited to the rest of this part of the Île de la Cité. The PALAIS DE JUSTICE itself is not a popular tourist destination, and for good reason; but since we have to enter its precincts to get to the Sainte Chapelle, we can at least have a glance inside. It is a soulless place of stone pillars and marble halls, with the echoing vestibules of official buildings where people's lives are disposed of. Its scale is designed to intimidate. Among its long corridors is the *chambre correctionelle*, where in one year, 1857, the French state managed to prosecute two of the greatest works of literature to come out of France in the nineteenth century: Flaubert's *Madame Bovary* and Baudelaire's *Les Fleurs du Mal*. Notice in the Grande Salle the monument to Berryer. The nineteenth-century lawyer looks dedicated both to the ideal of Justice and to his own importance. Whether he would have been pleased to see one of the accompanying allegorical figures resting her left foot on a tortoise is another matter.

Perhaps the main reward of a trudge round the law courts is to be found right at the end of the Galerie Duc, where we have an unusual view of the SAINTE CHA-PELLE. This miraculous little church, enclosed within the grounds of the Palais de Justice, dates from the mid thirteenth century. It was designed by the architect Pierre de Montreuil to house the Crown of Thorns, which St Louis had brought from Venice, where Baldwin of Constantinople had left it in pawn to Venetian merchants. After a brief stay in Notre-Dame the crown was duly installed in a reliquary above the high altar of the Sainte Chapelle. St Louis alone held the key and on festival days he would mount one of the two spiral staircases beside the altar, unlock the reliquary and display the crown to the congregation in the nave. During the Revolution the reliquary was melted down and the crown has since found its way back to the treasury of Notre-Dame.

The glory of the Sainte Chapelle is its stained glass. Standing in the upper chapel, which was reserved for the court and the royal family, we may not be much taken by the gilded statues that look down on us, but the richness of colour in these tall, slender windows is breathtaking. To see the windows set in plain stone rather than surrounded by the distracting decoration that was wished on the chapel in the nineteenth century would be an extraordinary experience. That we can see the place at all is a cause for gratitude. In May 1871 the Palais de Justice was in flames and the Sainte Chapelle had been drenched in paraffin. It was a merciful chance that left the work of the Communards unfinished.

Half-way along the quai des Orfèvres – so-called because it was the centre for jewellery in the seventeenth and eighteenth centuries – we can turn right to reach the place Dauphine, tucked away behind the pont Neuf. It is a seductive little spot which until 1874 was closed off by a third row of houses along what is now the rue de Harlay. This arrangement was destroyed to provide an open prospect of the uninspiring west front of the Palais de Justice. Only a few of the original seventeenth-century façades remain, but it is still a quiet, elegant little place, whose sandy triangle is dotted with trees and benches. A number of attractive restaurants make it an excellent spot to spend the middle of the day. Last time I was there an aged man playing a concertina and a couple of groups enjoying a lunchtime game of *boules* completed the atmosphere of old Paris.

From the place Dauphine one looks straight down the little rue Henri-Robert to the equestrian statue of Henri IV which stands in the middle of the

A typical Parisian drinking fountain in front of the busy flower market in the place Louis-Lépine.

pont Neuf. The most handsome of all Paris's bridges, the pont Neuf is also, in spite of its name, the oldest. Its first stone was laid by Henri III on the evening of 31 May 1578 in circumstances which led to its being popularly called the Bridge of Tears. A few weeks earlier three of the king's favourites, including the two most dearly loved, Quélus and Maugiron, had fought a ferocious duel with members of the Guise family. At the end of the duel two of the Guises were dead and one permanently crippled, two of the favourites were dead and Quélus mortally wounded. On the morning that the foundation stone of the pont Neuf was laid Henri III had attended the funeral service for Quélus and Maugiron. He arrived at the ceremony for the new bridge in deepest mourning, his tears matched by the pouring rain.

After this unhappy start, the fortunes of the bridge improved. Completed under Henri IV, it rapidly became one of the liveliest spots in Paris. Not only did it have raised footpaths at either side, so that pedestrians could escape the mud flung up by passing carriages, it was also unencumbered with the usual shops and houses. Earlier bridges had been built up in much the same way as streets – houses and shops stacked high along the sides – with the result that it was imposs- ible to see the river as one passed over it. The pont Neuf opened up new pros- pects. It is difficult for us now to appreciate how superbly broad it must have seemed to the inhabitants of Paris's narrow, lightless streets in the seventeenth century. Before long it was lined with booths and side-shows. Doctors, dentists, art dealers, actors, mountebanks – everyone staked a claim. The daily ferment of activity made the pont Neuf a scene of traffic jams that would look formidable even by the standards of the twentieth century.

The figure of Henri IV, overlooking a square bay at the centre of the bridge, has weathered a number of storms in the past four hundred years. The original bronze statue, which had been cast in Florence, sank off the coast of Sardinia on its way back from Leghorn in 1613. A year later it was recovered and brought to this site on the pont Neuf, where it survived until 1792, when anti-royalist feeling reached such a pitch that even France's best-loved monarch ended up in the melting pot. Napoleon had it in mind to embellish the empty site with a huge obe- lisk, inscribed '*l'Empereur Napoléon au Peuple Français*', which would perhaps have meant much the same as '*Le Peuple Français à l'Empereur Napoléon*', but as things turned out, it was the king who had the last laugh. In 1818 the statue of Napoleon on top of the column in the place Vendôme (together with another statue of him from Boulogne) was melted down to be recast – as a new statue of Henri IV for the pont Neuf. And here it has remained.

From behind the statue we can walk down to the pretty little triangular gar- den at the tip of the island which forms the square du Vert Galant. Alongside are moored some of the Seine's increasingly huge *bateaux mouches*, waiting for their freight of tourists. The name of Vert Galant – 'sparky old chap' might be a rough equivalent – was given to Henri IV in honour of his amorous proclivities, and this is his square. In the days before the pont Neuf, the Île de la Cité tapered away into a series of lesser islands which were later consolidated into the present arrange-

ment. As you begin to climb back up to the bridge, you might notice a small plaque between the two flights of steps which indicates that it was here that Jacques de Molay, the last Grand Master of the Knights Templar, was burned at the stake on 18 March 1314.

Before we leave the islands, there is one more place to visit, not the kind of spot one is likely to pass without noticing. For 600 years the CONCIERGERIE has loured across the Seine towards the place du Châtelet, a massive witness to the changing scenes of Paris's history. Even today, peopled as it is by tourists, there is something oppressive about the great Salle des Gens d'Armes, with its medieval pillars, low vault, and high, barred windows. Behind us as we enter are the Tour de César, where Ravaillac was imprisoned after murdering Henri IV, and the Tour d'Argent, where Damiens was imprisoned after his attempt on the life of Louis XV. These were just two from a long line of eminent, and for the most part doomed, prisoners who have surveyed the grim walls that surround us. The list includes many whose names are already known to everyone, some who will become more familiar in the course of these pages, among them Danton, Desmoulins, Robespierre, Marie-Antoinette and the Marquise de Brinvilliers.

Only a small part of the building is open to the public, but an effort has been made over the past few years to give some sort of coherence to one's visit. Explanatory notes and pictures, historical reconstructions and a video presentation all attempt, with limited success, to bring the stones of the Conciergerie to life. Apart from the fourteenth-century kitchens with their four huge chimneys, most of what is to be seen takes us back to the period of the Revolution. Upstairs, a number of rooms have been arranged in the form of tableaux, showing the more or less vile conditions in which different categories of prisoner were kept. A reconstructed cell on the ground floor evokes the circumstances in which Marie-Antoinette passed her final days. Nearby, there is the wretched little Cour des Femmes, surrounded on all sides by high walls, where other female prisoners could get an occasional glimpse of the sky. In brief, the Conciergerie offers the sort of record of human misery that few can resist.

The quai de l'Horloge, running alongside the prison, derives its name from Paris's first public clock, which was set in the Tour de l'Horloge in the fourteenth century. During the Revolution this quay was the site of one particularly grisly trade to which the guillotine had given an unexpected boost: the sale of hair to supply the eighteenth-century taste for elegant wigs.

We can leave the Île de la Cité by crossing the pont au Change, where in the Middle Ages we would have come to change our money after arriving in Paris. On the other side, the place du Châtelet has only a stone plaque beside the Chambre des Notaires to recall the dreaded fortress which gave it its name.

I suppose no one has ever felt a lifting of the spirits on first sight of the boulevard de Sébastopol, which leads out of the square to the north. Subsequent visits are unlikely to change the impression. It is a wide, dreary street laid out in the middle of the nineteenth century by Haussmann with the specific intention of making life difficult for urban revolutionaries. The tangle of narrow streets

OPPOSITE *Lemot's bronze equestrian statue of Paris's favourite monarch, Henri IV, which has stood in the middle of the pont Neuf since 1818.*

through which it cut had been too easy to barricade during the insurrections of 1848. What was wanted was a clear field of fire that could be swept by a company of troops. The boulevard de Sébastopol provided this, but not much else.

More interesting by far is the area just to the west, once the site of the old markets, now a showpiece of modern Paris. My own feelings about this eruption of steel and glass in the centre of the city are mixed. As the years pass, there will be fewer and fewer people who feel the prickings of nostalgia for what was sacrificed to Pompidou's grandiose scheme, but I remember with a thrill of regret the exhilarating atmosphere of LES HALLES in the hours around daybreak when the real business of the place used to be conducted.

That said, it must be admitted that what replaced Baltard's pavilions could have been very much worse. In the end I must count myself a reluctant convert to the new order. The underground shopping precinct is of little interest. Reminiscent of the miniature cities that have grown up at subway stations in Tokyo, it offers the usual display of teenage clothes-shops and sterile cafés. It is perhaps the most appropriate site in Paris, of all their many sites, for the smart, light, leafy new red-and-yellow McDonald's that has opened there. Above ground, the prospect seems to me infinitely more pleasing. As you wander round the new complex and into the park that has been created to the west of it, there is much to enjoy. Near the Porte du Berger, the terrace above the multi-coloured mosaic waterfall offers a fine view towards the dome of the Bourse du Commerce – the last surviving relic of the old Halles. Below you, a restored merry-go-round from 1872, complete with charming wooden horses and coaches, circles to the traditional music of the fair-ground, suggesting an older world that seems remarkably untroubled by its ultra-modern setting.

From the other side of the park, near the Porte du Louvre, there is an equally attractive view across the centre of Paris towards the yawning funnels of the Pompidou Centre. The allée Louis Aragon offers a pleasant vantage point. Just below it is a group of glass pyramids enclosing an unexpected forest of tropical vegetation, and behind the pyramids are banks of flowers. The Jardins des Halles, and indeed the whole development, can change appearance radically with the seasons. In winter it can all look rather drab, in summer a delight. There is, in any case, a redeeming sense that the area has been laid out for the benefit of the people who will use it rather than to fulfill an architect's dream or a town-planner's notions of economy. It is a work of variety and imagination which continually throws up new perspectives and light-hearted diversions – an unobtrusive fountain here, a work of sculpture there, an arch of flowers in the distance. As so often in Paris – and so rarely in London – one has the impression of things done simply because people might find them pretty, amusing or encouraging. It is this concern with the quality of life in the city that increasingly distinguishes Paris from its neighbour across the Channel.

One undoubted beneficiary of the upheavals of the past few years has been the church of SAINT-EUSTACHE. Built between 1532 and 1637, it now dominates the area and shows its elegant network of buttresses to splendid advantage.

OPPOSITE *The Préfecture de Police on the corner of the quai des Orfèvres is typical of much nineteenth-century Parisian official architecture.*

The church of Saint-Eustache dominates the edge of the new gardens laid out on the site of the old markets of Les Halles.

At the corner of the rue Montorgueil and the rue Rambuteau it towers above its surroundings, an engaging mixture of the medieval and the Renaissance, and seems in the past decade to have been gaining a new lease of life, more visited both by sightseers and by concert-goers. Its newly acquired grandeur reflects a distinguished past. Richelieu was baptized here, as was the future Mme de Pompadour. Molière was both baptized and, in spite of opposition from the local priest, buried here with considerable pomp. La Fontaine was another literary figure to be buried in the church. Its musical tradition is equally impressive, since it was here that Berlioz conducted the first performance of his *Te Deum* and Liszt his *Messe Solenelle*.

Inside, you will find Le Brun's lavish tomb of Colbert, as well as Pigalle's Virgin and Child and a sixteenth-century statue of St John the Evangelist. Less known is the delightful polychrome sculpture almost opposite the south entrance. This is Raymond Mason's *The Departure of the Fruit and Vegetables from the Heart of Paris on 28 February 1969*. Against the background of Saint-Eustache it depicts the familiar figures of Les Halles, the porters and the *fortes femmes*, all of them laden with the colourful produce of the old markets. With their tough, battered, vinous faces, they look stolidly towards the new destination as they make their way out of the city. It is a touching tribute to a world that disappeared with the demolition of Les Halles. As Mason put it, 'In truth, the market of the Halles Centrales was the last image of the Natural in the City. It is now a Paradise Lost.'

The new dispensation in Les Halles has its failures, of course, and I am inclined to think that Julio Silva's much publicised sculpture *Pyégmalion* in the place Carrée is one of them. Its ugliness is aggravated by the awful certainty that the whole thing bears some symbolic meaning. Far more successful is the use which has been made of the sixteenth-century Fontaine des Innocents. This lovely fountain looks almost like a temple to fountains, its source enclosed in a tabernacle from which water cascades down tiers of steps with a refreshing sound. Since it is now the focal point for skate-boarders, guitarists, drunks, pic-nickers and sightseers, the base of the fountain is surrounded by the usual debris of tourism, but in spite of the refuse and the racket, the fountain itself somehow manages to remain an oddly restful spot around which people can comfortably sit and talk and stare at the water.

Running alongside this playground is the rue des Innocents, where in a couple of the shops you can still see remains of some of the arches of the notorious cemetery which occupied this site from the tenth century to the eighteenth. It was thought to be a property of the earth in the Cimetière des Innocents that it could devour human flesh at an extraordinary pace; a body interred here was reckoned to be stripped of flesh within nine days. When the graves were opened up to receive a fresh batch of occupants, the bones of previous tenants were removed. These were stored in a series of galleries with which the walls of the cemetery were furnished. By the eighteenth century the ossuaries were crammed to over-flowing, though this apparently did nothing to dim the popularity of the spot. In spite of the jumble of bones, the regular deliveries of corpses and the appalling stench, the cemetery of the Innocents was much in vogue among idlers, street traders, pimps, prostitutes, anyone who wanted to take the air in the city centre. It was only in 1780, after a house in the rue de la Lingerie had collapsed into one of the huge common graves among a welter of half-decomposed corpses, that the cemetery was finally closed.

Leading northwards from the square des Innocents is the ancient rue Saint-Denis, much frequented by the kind of figures who might once have been seen touting for custom in the cemetery. The street is now a cheerful combination of carnival and sleaze, where gimmicky restaurants set out their tables beside sand-wich boards offering a variety of voyeuristic treats, all of them '*super hard*'. Further on, the pleasures become less voyeuristic and more practical.

A favourite station for the *filles* of the *quartier* is the ancient fountain – or rather the remains of it – on the corner of the rue Greneta. Fountains such as this, play-ing wine or milk, would greet new kings on their triumphal entry into Paris through the arch of the seventeenth-century PORTE SAINT-DENIS at the end of the street. (As it happens, the last monarch to enter the city in this way was the very unFrench Queen Victoria, when she came in 1855 to visit the Exhibition.)

The pyramids on the arch are adorned with a quantity of grimy sculpture, much appreciated by the pigeons, celebrating Louis XIV's victories in Germany and Holland. Much the most attractive piece is the large lion's head that hangs down from the top of the arch with its tongue extended, as it is apparently gasping for a drink.

From the pyramids on the face of the triumphal arch we can turn to a quite different echo of Egypt by walking down the rue d'Aboukir, which is lined with the cheap clothes shops that are the hallmark of this area. A short detour via the rue d'Alexandrie will enable us to take the glass-covered passageway into the place du Caire. All these names, like others in the district, belong to the era of Napoleon's victories in Egypt, which brought in their wake a mania for things Egyptian, reflected in contemporary fashions in clothes, furniture, architectural ornament and the like. The place du Caire itself is an unremarkable little square more or less fully occupied by a public lavatory, a clutch of telephones, a group of frail trees and a slightly disquieting sculpture by Olivier Brice. Even so, readers of a romantic turn will think it worth a visit for its associations with the world of Hugo's *Notre-Dame de Paris*. For centuries this was the site of the most famous of Paris's Cours des Miracles, enclaves in the heart of the city where criminals and beggars had established a separate kingdom beyond the reach of the law. Each night when the mutilated beggars returned to this place, their afflictions would be miraculously sloughed off: the lame would walk and the blind see, the crippled would be made whole. Living under their own king, with their own rules and their own language, they defied any interference from the more respectable sections of society, until an energetic police chief in the seventeenth century at last managed to suppress them. Today, no doubt for other reasons, the police tend still to be much in evidence in the district.

The street which runs down to the left just beyond the place du Caire becomes after a few yards the rue du Montorgueil, heralded by an arch announcing the Marché Montorgueil. This ancient street has been around in one form or another since the thirteenth century and its market is a colourful scene of fish, fruit, meats, cheeses and flowers overflowing the pavement. A picture by Monet of the rue Montorgueil *en fête*, hung with flags on 30 June 1878, can be seen in the Musée d'Orsay.

A short disance from the church of Saint-Eustache the street crosses the rue Etienne-Marcel, and we can turn aside briefly at this point for a glance at the TOUR DE JEAN SANS PEUR. In the context 'sans Peur' could hardly be less appropriate. The tower was built in 1408 because Jean sans Peur, the Duke of Burgundy, was terrified of being murdered in revenge for his assassination of the Duke of Orléans the previous year. The precaution was only moderately successful; his assassins merely murdered him elsewhere. We can reach the tower by turning left along Etienne-Marcel until we reach number 20, just beyond the rue Française. Scheduled for restoration, the tower is a rugged piece of work, square and stubborn, that even in its heyday can have been none too comfortable. It has the look of a building that has survived much.

OPPOSITE *The church of Saint-Eustache took so long to build – from 1532 to 1640 – that parts of it were out of fashion before it was finished and it is a unique mixture of late gothic and renaissance elements.*

The distinctive dome of the mid eighteenth-century Bourse de Commerce, once the Corn Exchange, is still a landmark on the corner of Les Halles.

At the end of the rue Montorgueil we are back beside Saint-Eustache with the BOURSE DU COMMERCE over on our right. It is not just the Bourse itself that is worth having a look at. Rising beside it is the tower known as the *colonne astrologique*. It is a curious object – a Doric column with nothing to support except a metal cage perched on top. Built in the sixteenth century for Catherine de' Medici, the column has no discernible function and for this reason as much as any other it has been assumed that the superstitious queen must have used it for the purposes of astrology.

South of the Bourse du Commerce we run into the early stages of the rue Saint-Honoré, just at the point where it crosses the rue de l'Arbre-Sec. The 'sapless tree' that gave this street its name is a grimly humorous reference to the gallows which once stood at this intersection. Marked only by a modest drinking fountain from the reign of Louis XVI, it seems a fairly insignificant spot today, but over the years it has enjoyed a certain celebrity. Apart from being a place of execution, it was also the place where in the seventeenth century clumsy servants suffered the punishment of having their ears cropped. It seems that the executioner usually cut off the left ear for preference on the grounds that there was a nerve in it connected to the organs of generation, which, once cut, made it impossible for the man to bring any more clumsy servants into the world. As the historian Jacques Hillairet remarked, for a servant to have both his ears intact was in those days the equivalent of a first-class reference.

For some reason this crossroads was a frequent scene of public disorders, most notably in the summer of 1648. A clash here, sparked off by the arrest of a member of Parliament, started the five years of turbulence known as the Fronde. This was basically an attempt by a shifting alliance of Parliament, the nobility and the people to challenge the power of the monarchy. It was a messy and disorganized business that repeatedly plunged Paris into turmoil. Little was achieved, but the Fronde had one important consequence. By the time Louis XIV established himself in power, he had learned the lesson that was to shape French political history for the next century. No one, at any level, was to be allowed a base from which to challenge the power of the king. *L'État, c'est moi.*

Before moving down towards the river, have a look at the sleek modern pharmacy a couple of doors along the rue Saint-Honoré at number 115. It has been there since at least the early eighteenth century when it was owned by an apothecary called Bernard Derosne. If you look at the inscription above the door on the left, you can still make out his name under the announcement of Produits Chimiques. According to legend, it was from here that the Comte de Fersen procured invisible ink which he used in his correspondence with Marie-Antoinette. His adoration of her gave rise to numerous stories of an illicit affair, but all that can be proved is a fanatical devotion which was at least partly responsible for the absurd escape attempt from the Palace of the Tuileries that sealed her fate.

At its southern end, the rue de l'Arbre-Sec passes alongside the apse of the church of SAINT-GERMAIN-L'AUXERROIS. Walk round to the west front of the church, facing the place du Louvre, and you can examine the magnificent porch, built by Jean Gaussel in the first half of the fifteenth century. Notice, in particular, the figure of St Geneviève in the central bay, with an especially persistent devil at her right shoulder, trying unsuccessfully to blow out the flame of her candle. (She is associated with this church because it was Bishop St Germain of Auxerre who first inspired her to dedicate her life to God.) The bell tower that stands beside this west façade of the church belongs to the nineteenth century, but as you walk back towards the rue de l'Arbre-Sec, you will pass the original bell tower on the south side of the church. It was from here, on the night of 23–24 August 1572, that the signal was given for the start of the massacre of St Bartholomew. Of the three bells which rang out on that night the largest still remains in the tower.

At the end of the rue de l'Arbre-Sec stands one of Paris's most famous department stores. The Samaritaine took its name from that of a water pump, decorated with an image of the woman of Samaria, which used to be under an arch of the nearby pont Neuf. The store is today an empire in its own right, though in places a slightly cluttered one, losing ground, perhaps, to the more stylish layout of some of its competitors.

We can finish our walk by turning left onto the quai de la Mégisserie, which will bring us back to the pont au Change and the place du Châtelet. The quay offers a lively walk between clucking chickens, cages of rabbits, tanks of terrapins and lines of plants and flowers. Alternatively, we can cross the road to enjoy a pleasant view over the Seine to the turrets of the Conciergerie. We are lucky to be walking here in the twentieth century. In earlier times, when it was the site of the public slaughterhouse, one might have made a considerable detour to avoid it. With ironic appropriateness it later became the place where army recruiting officers conducted their business, trying, with the help of local prostitutes, to lure unwary youths into the wretched life of a soldier.

For us a more cheerful prospect awaits, as we reach the square again and subside into one of the chairs outside the Café Au Vieux Châtelet.

The fifteenth-century high gothic porch of the church of Saint-Germain-l'Auxerrois.

2
Central Paris

....

THE LOUVRE *to* THE ARC DE TRIOMPHE

It is one of the pleasures of being in Paris to sit on a bench on the pont des Arts, empty one's mind and gaze along the Seine towards Notre-Dame. Of all the city's bridges it offers the most bewitching prospect. When it opened in the early nineteenth century, its users had to pay for the amenity with a toll of one sou. Today we can stroll on towards the PALAIS DU LOUVRE untaxed by anyone but the pavement artists.

What we look at from the bridge is the splendid palace façade that fronts the Seine; what we look at once we have penetrated behind the façade is something quite different. There seems little point in raging against I.M. Pei's giant glass pyramid, which now dominates the Cour Napoléon. For better or worse, the palace has been hacked about by one monarch after another for most of its 800-year history. Inside the museum we can still see part of the original fortress that Philippe-Auguste built at the end of the twelfth century, and if we walk round the outside, we shall be making our way past a series of additions and reconstructions that range from François I to Napoleon III. It was merely a freak that had left the Louvre practically unchanged for the past century.

By night the illuminated pyramid is spectacular, by day I find it less successful. This is partly because it relegates the two fountains playing beside it to insignificance, partly because its framework of taut steel wires makes it semi-opaque. If we could see through it from one side of the courtyard to the other, the effect would be less intrusive. Moreover, the fact that it is constructed of glass may in itself turn out to be something of a hazard. It is one of the great advantages of stone that it accommodates the attentions of passing pigeons with rather more dignity than glass. At the moment, intrepid mountaineers, secured by slings, are employed to keep the surface of the pyramid looking more or less pristine. In twenty years' time, who is to say?

The business of getting into the museum can be more or less painful depending on the time of day and season of the year. In high season there are huge

OPPOSITE *I.M. Pei's giant glass pyramid adds a note of glamour to this romantic view from the Cour Napoleon of the Palais du Louvre.*

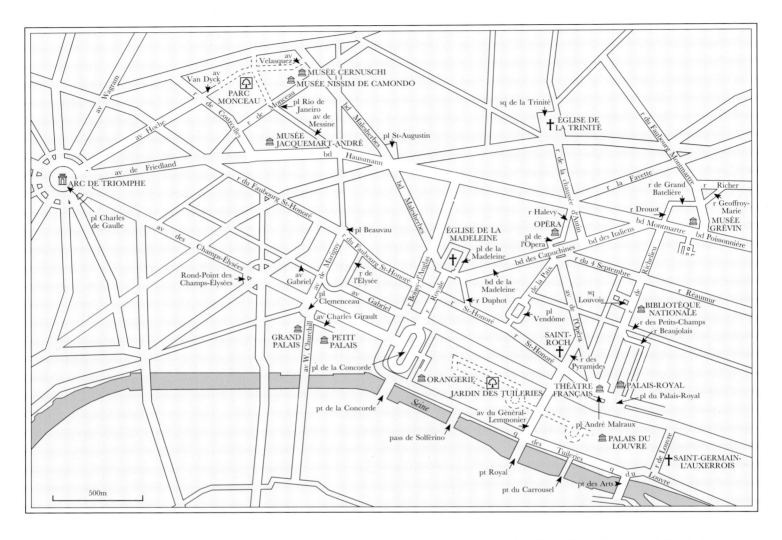

CENTRAL PARIS

queues snaking right the way round the Cour Napoléon. And that is just to get into the pyramid; further queues await you at the ticket office. I suppose the ideal time for a visit would be the early hours of the morning in mid-winter, but since that is not an option the best plan is to buy in advance a *carte des musées*, which entitles you to access by a side-door without the need to queue. Once inside the pyramid, you will find that the new central concourse looks more like an airport terminal than an art gallery, but at least the problem of finding one's way around has been greatly simplified. Stairways lead off to each of the three wings of the museum – Richelieu, Denon and Sully – and with the help of the free plan it is fairly easy to work out where everything is. A certain amount of reorganization still remains to be done, but for the first time, at least in my experience, the visitor is in a position to grasp the layout of the place and to understand how this vast and disparate collection is organized.

'Limit yourself to a few exhibits and then go back another time' is the excellent advice one is usually given. Unfortunately, repeated visits require almost as much stamina as one long haul. The flesh is weak, and most people, however good their intentions, end up visiting the Louvre once and then finding other things to do for the rest of their stay. With this in mind I would advise you not to put off anything you desperately want to see – with the possible exception of the *Mona Lisa*, which is surrounded by people, encased in a cabinet of bullet-proof glass and altogether more wonderful in imagination than in rather sordid reality. My recipe for an enjoyable visit, perhaps on a Monday or Wednesday evening when the museum stays open late, would be to spend the first hour strolling around in search of old favourites. The collection is so overwhelming that any choice will be arbitrary. In the long gallery, for example, do you make first for Mantegna's *Crucifixion*, Pisanello's *Portrait of a Princess of the Este Family*, Watteau's *Pilgrimage to the Isle of Cythera*, or perhaps Lorenzo di Credi's little *Annunciation*? And what of the endless miles of faience, where a few striking scenes of pornography are usually kept in the decent obscurity of the drawers under the main cabinets? Would you want to leave the side-galleries without finding Vermeer's *Lacemaker*, or the Egyptian galleries without spending a moment or two in front of the engaging polychrome hippopotamus? Where do you begin, where do you end? As long as one does not try it with an empty stomach, it can all be quite fun; but in truth it is not a place for aesthetic contemplation. Large expanses of the gallery are tourist motorways where the crowds file doggedly along, incurious of the paintings to right and left. Always the crowds. Italians in holiday mood have themselves photographed with heads appearing over the top of headless statues; harassed group leaders wave banners, sticks, umbrellas, fans; tall Americans wield video cameras while their wives speak suitably awe-struck commentaries at the side; children, bored to distraction, ready themselves for violence. The effect of all this swarming life among the silent statues and paintings of antiquity is dizzying. It's magnificent but it's not an art gallery, or not what most of us think of as one.

So for our second hour we shall turn our back on it. This is simply done. As simply as walking up to the second floor of the Pavillon Sully. I have been here in mid-August, when the rest of the museum is a swirling mass of humanity, and found just a handful of lonely souls who had been led up here by their rented cassette guides. For the moment there is little to be seen on the second floor of either the Richelieu or Denon wings of the museum, so that this area of French paintings in Sully is effectively isolated from the rest of the collection. And yet the display is stunning. Apart from the École de Fontainebleau, we have paintings by Clouet, Poussin and Claude, as well as a wonderful series of portraits, including Richelieu by Philippe de Champaigne, the Chancellier Séguier by Le Brun, and Hyacinthe Rigaud's sardonic image of Louis XIV, whose elaborate pose and mean, suspicious face offer a study in rancid self-esteem. In this same part of the museum we can also see George de la Tour's *Le Tricheur*, in which a rich young gull is being parted from his money by a confederacy of card-sharp, prostitute and waitress. It is a brilliantly realized scene of side-long glances and corruption.

Jacques Louis David's The Consecration of the Emperor Napoleon and Coronation of the Empress Josephine, 2 December, 1804, *painted between 1806 and 1807, is one of the great neoclassical paintings in the Louvre.*

All in all, until the next upheaval redisposes the paintings of the Louvre, this seems to me the section of the museum to head for, and indeed the only section of it where you are likely to be more conscious of the paintings than the crowds.

After tramping the corridors of the Louvre a burst of fresh air is essential, and fortunately the JARDIN DES TUILERIES is ready to hand. Named for the tiles which used to be made from the clay hereabouts, these gardens, laid out in their present form in the seventeenth century by André Le Nôtre, were for long an aristocratic preserve, much in favour with courtiers and their catamites but out of bounds to soldiers and servants. Even 150 years ago it was still forbidden to enter certain parts of them in working clothes or carrying a parcel. 'This is an enclosure of all sweet sights and smells, a concentration of elegance,' wrote the essayist William Hazlitt in 1824. 'The rest of the world is barbarous to this "paradise of dainty devices", where the imagination is spellbound.' I would hesitate to go quite as far as Hazlitt, but I like these gardens – in summer it is pleasant to sit under the chestnut trees with a drink, watching the people and the pigeons and thinking how lucky one is to be here and nowhere else; in winter I like the nakedness of the place and the cold stone statues, which look best of all in the early morning when they are topped with new snow.

Running alongside the Tuileries is the arcaded rue de Rivoli, with the Hôtel Meurice at number 228. Much in vogue among the visiting English of the nineteenth century, including Dickens and Thackeray, it was notable more recently as the headquarters of the German General von Choltitz when he was Commandant of Occupied Paris. It was here that he gave up his sword and pistol on the afternoon of 25 August, 1944. He had only taken over the command a fortnight earlier and his orders were quite specific: if any German troops came under fire, he was to 'destroy as wide an area of Paris as possible, demolishing the bridges and taking the most severe and bloody reprisals'. In the event, he disobeyed the orders and lived to return to Paris twenty years later, when he was photographed, an honoured guest, beside a plaque on the wall of the old Gare Montparnasse where he had signed the orders to local German troop leaders to surrender.

Formal elegance in the empty pathways of the Tuileries in the early spring, looking across from the Seine towards the rue de Rivoli.

The church on the left when you reach the rue Saint-Honoré is SAINT-ROCH, which deserves a mention as the burial place of Corneille and Diderot. Since we have just left the Tuileries, you might also like to have a glance, while you are here, at the finely sculpted bust of Le Nôtre by Coysevox. The wrinkled lip and Roman nose bespeak a man who did not take kindly to interference in his projects. Saint-Roch is also interesting for a less conventional reason. The front of the church is pock-marked with the legacy of Napoleon's 'whiff of grapeshot', by which, on 5 October, 1795, he dispersed the rebels threatening the Convention. It was, according to Thomas Carlyle, the decisive moment at which 'the thing we specifically call *French Revolution* is blown into space'.

A few yards along the rue Saint-Honoré in the other direction, Davioud's twin fountains announce what is now called the place André-Malraux after the author of *La condition humaine*, who later became France's Minister of Culture under de Gaulle. Dominating the east side of the square are the buildings of the THÉÂTRE FRANÇAIS which gave the square its earlier name. The theare opened on the night of 30 May, 1799 with a performance of Corneille's *Le Cid*, a play that has remained a showpiece for French classical acting. I confess I have rarely set foot in the place in recent years. My first visit – to see Rostand's *Cyrano de Bergerac*, one of the company perennials – lingers in my memory largely for the look of incredulous disgust which fixed itself on the face of the *ouvreuse* when, after she had shown me to my seat, I innocently pressed into her outstretched hand my torn-off ticket stub rather than the *pourboire* she was expecting. Since then I have seen other plays and learned to manage the business more urbanely, but on the whole I am still inclined to feel that an evening in Paris can be better spent. The conscientious tourist will, however, at least want to get as far as the foyer to see the chair in which Molière was sitting when he was taken ill during a performance of *Le Malade imaginaire* and Houdon's fine bust of Voltaire.

Before retreating into the gardens of the Palais-Royal, we might just take a brief look at the Louvre des Antiquaires on the far side of the square. This newly designed complex of antique shops is much too glossy and well ordered to offer anything in the way of bargains, but for the window shopper or the person of means there are some attractive articles on sale. (Less publicized but equally welcome on occasion are the excellent free lavatories.)

The gardens of the nearby PALAIS-ROYAL are a place for which I feel a continuing fondness. The city's tumultuous surge into the twentieth century seems somehow to have left them behind. Surrounded by the noisy, bustling lives of the city centre, they remain for most of the time a quiet, rather lonely spot, the haunt of solitary knitters, quiet conversationalists and dignified promenaders. But if there are few people to keep one company, there are plenty of ghosts – from Camille Desmoulins, who here delivered the speech which inspired the march on the Bastille a day later, to the poet Gérard de Nerval, who in gentler times used to walk his pet lobster here, attached by a blue ribbon. Lobsters, he explained, had a particular place in his affections 'because they are calm, serious and know the secrets of the sea'.

It is only in the past century and a half that such respectable pursuits have been possible in the gardens of the Palais-Royal. Before that, they could hardly have presented a greater contast to their modern tranquillity. Built for Richelieu in the seventeenth century, the palace eventually passed into the hands of Philippe d'Orléans who gave it its present aspect shortly before the Revolution. Heavily in debt, he constructed the arcades round three sides of the garden and then rented out the resulting space to a variety of cafés, restaurants, shops, gambling dens and brothels. The whole area was seething with prostitutes, who conducted their business among puppet-theatres, freak-shows, pornographers, political pamphleteers, gamesters, tricksters and sellers of practically anything one might want. (It was at a cutler's shop in the Galerie de Valois, on the site of what is now number 177, that Charlotte Corday bought the knife with which later that day she stabbed Marat.) For foreigners, particularly Englishmen, it was a promised land where everything that made Paris desirable could be had for the asking in one place. During the Napoleonic wars one English epicure was heard to remark that as soon as peace was declared, 'he would give himself the happiness of passing six weeks in the Palais-Royal without once going out of its gates'.

It is probably too much to expect that the Palais-Royal will retain its quiet charm for long. Already the main courtyard has been embellished by the mint-humbug style contributions of the sculptor Daniel Buren. Reminiscent of lopped tree trunks, these black and white striped pillars might have been a cheerful addition to the parvis of La Défense; here they look merely foolish. For the moment, though, we can still stroll down the sandy paths between the trees, or along the shady arcades, lined with offices and a few old shops that look as though they would have no trouble accommodating characters out of a novel by Honoré de Balzac. If we have made a reservation and taken out a second mortgage, we might even sink into the atmosphere of the late eighteenth century and have lunch at Le Grand Véfour.

In the Galerie de Beaujolais at the northern end of the gardens, a plaque marks the house where Colette spent the last sixteen years of her life. Just beneath it runs the passage du Perron, which passes alongside an eccentric little shop, highly characteristic of the Palais-Royal, specializing in music boxes. The passageway opens into the rue de Beaujolais, where we can turn left towards another passage that takes us through to the rue de Richelieu within sight of Visconti's monument to Molière. The dramatist sits under an elaborate arch, looking towards the spot where his house once stood, at number 40. Diderot died across the street, at number 39, in 1784.

A few yards away is the square Louvois, with at its centre the younger Visconti's grand, and slighty grandiose, fountain, composed of statues representing the rivers Seine, Loire, Saône and Garonne. Underneath the statues four deplorably plump *putti* ride on spouting fish. The whole thing is a little absurd, but its streams of water falling from different heights through the sunlight create a beguiling display. Until the early nineteenth century this was the site of the opera, which was moved after the Duc de Berry was assassinated just outside it in 1820.

Opposite the fountain is the entrance to the BIBLIOTHÈQUE NATIONALE. The idea for a national library, or as it was then, a royal library, dates back to François I, who established it in the sixteenth century. Since 1724 it has been housed here in the Hôtel Tubeuf, part of the former home of Cardinal Mazarin. It does not rank high on most people's list of tourist spots, but the Musée du Cabinet des Médailles et Antiques, housed in the same building, repays a visit, if only for the sight of Charlemagne's chess set. These superb pieces were not, alas, offered to Charlemagne by Haroun al Raschid, Calif of Baghdad, as the legend claims; they belong to the eleventh century and probably came from somewhere near Salerno in southern Italy. Particularly attractive are the little pawns, looking apprehensively over their huge shields, and the ponderous elephants which take the part of bishops. Among other items in the museum you can see an unusual third-century Roman coin stamped with the image of Elagabalus. For an emperor who was even more depraved than the notorious Caligula, he looks quite personable, but then honesty has never been the best policy for imperial image-makers. Also on display for lovers of legend is the so-called 'Throne of Dagobert', a wooden seat which may be something of a disappointment to all but the highly imaginative.

The top end of the rue de Richelieu runs into the boulevard Montmartre, and we can take our pick from a number of neighbouring attractions. I have never been able to work up much enthusiasm for waxworks, but if waxy tableaux of scenes from the Revolution and life in the *belle époque* are to your taste, the MUSÉE GRÉVIN is only a few yards along the street. Certainly we must look at the passage des Panoramas, which runs off the boulevard almost opposite the museum. Opened in 1800, it enjoyed great popularity in the nineteenth century as a centre for fashionable shops and cafés. Like the rest of the boulevard it has lost its claim to fashion now, but if you wish to sample the refinements of an earlier age you can still go to number 47 and have your *cartes de visite* engraved at Stern's. The passage, which took its name from the panoramas of capital cities that were on display here, became in 1817 one of the first thoroughfares to be lit by gas.

Anyone whose vision of Paris has been shaped by quaint images of dancing girls kicking up their heels on stage may want to stroll up to the rue Richer at this point. At number 32 the Folies-Bergère – '*Le Plus Célèbre Music Hall du Monde*', as it bills itself in lights outside – still offers the sort of entertainment for which Paris was once famous, though nowadays the theatre's patrons tend to be couples of a certain age dressed in rather self-conscious finery for a taste of the high life.

Perhaps better, since we are in the area, to check out the menu at Chartier's. This throwback to the 1900s – all dark wood and glinting brass – is not a restaurant for the leisured gourmet; good-humoured waiters are already muscling you off the seat by the time you are half-way through your coffee. But for a cheap meal in unforgettable surroundings, Chartier's is not to be missed. Patronized by a lively mixture of locals and tourists, it is situated at number 7 rue du Faubourg-Montmartre, and if you get there much after seven o'clock you will unfortunately be able to spot it in advance by the queue waiting outside the door.

OPPOSITE *The younger Visconti's Fontaine Louvois was erected in the square opposite the Bibliothèque Nationale in 1844.*

As we turn back towards the boulevard des Italiens, we shall pass quite close to Paris's main auction room, the Nouveau Drouot at number 9 rue Drouot. Even if you have no buying or selling to do, it is worth having a look at the new building whose façade is a startling display of metallic geometry. It might well spoil some people's lunch, but I quite like it. The fountain that dribbles down the corner of the building seems an admirable idea, but someone clearly needs to increase the miserly volume of water.

Heading westward down the boulevard des Italiens, we are now on what were once known as the *grands boulevards*, constructed under Louis XIV along the line of the old sixteenth-century ramparts. Today this is a fairly charmless section of the city, best adapted to rainy afternoons, but in the nineteenth century it was the centre of fashionable Paris, where the dandies flaunted their impeccable cravattes, and the *lions* quizzed passers-by from their café tables. No airline offices on

Jean Beraud's, The boulevard des Capucines and Vaudeville Theatre, *of 1889, shows the typical character of the area in the late nineteenth century.*

The façade of the nineteenth-century church of La Trinité seen from across the square.

the boulevard then, no cinemas, no McDonald's, no Pizza Huts. The nearest equivalent would perhaps be the Via Veneto in Rome in the days of Fellini's *Dolce Vita*, a street of glamorous cafés where the fashionable went to be stared at and the less fashionable went to stare. Tortoni's, the café Riche, the café Anglais and the café de Paris all set out their tables along these pavements; the gilded balconies of the old Maison Dorée can still be seen at number 20. When people speak of the nineteenth-century life of the boulevard, it is a fair bet that this is the boulevard they had in mind.

Before pressing on along the boulevard des Capucines, we must make a small, though not necessarily brief, detour up the chaussée d'Antin. At the end of the prospect is the bizarre nineteenth-century façade of the church of the TRINITÉ, but what we are actually going to visit is one of Paris's great department stores. The Galeries Lafayette started as a modest shop in 1895 and might

Charles Garnier's Opera House might now seem over-ornate but was the height of Second-Empire fashion when it was built.

have stayed that way if the owner had not had the vision to develop a new kind of consumer service. The prices here were fixed, customers could stroll in and have a look without any pressure to buy, and the store was willing to exchange goods after sale. The success of this revolution can be seen in the massive complex that now spreads itself across both sides of the chaussée. Even if you don't like shopping and don't like department stores, you might still want to spend a few minutes in the Galeries Lafayette. With its central area rising tier by tier towards the cupola of multi-coloured glass, it has the style that people expect of Paris.

Nearby stands another example of Parisian style, in its way as grand as anything in the city. The OPÉRA is a magnificent tribute to the taste and values of the Second Empire. Begun in 1862, to the designs of the architect Charles Garnier, it had to survive war and revolution before it was finally completed in 1875. The difficulties were formidable, the cost huge and the result spectacular. But times have changed; the profusion of gilt and marble and the lavish allegorical statuary attract fewer admirers today than they did a hundred years ago. There is somehow a flaw in the whole project, perhaps symbolically revealed by the fact that in spite of its size and elaboration, this enormous opera house actually accommodates relatively few spectators. With its sweeping staircase and vast corridors, it is a place where one goes to see and be seen rather than to concern oneself with what is happening on the stage. Among its other distinctions, this was the original haunt of Leroux's phantom.

To reach the place Vendôme we can simply walk down the rue de la Paix, perhaps turning aside for a quick drink in Harry's New York Bar at 5, rue Daunou. Frequented by Hemingway and Fitzgerald, Harry's claims to be the birthplace of the Bloody Mary. A sign in the window, announcing the address as 'Sank Roo Doe Noo', provides an *aide-mémoire* for customers with limited French.

The place Vendôme, at the far end of the rue de la Paix, is one of the glories of Paris. Ringed by beautiful hôtels almost all of which were built in the first couple of decades of the eighteenth century, it shares with the place des Vosges a splendid sense of architectural harmony. Standing at the base of the column we can cast an eye over some of its most famous hôtels. Best known of all is, of course, number 15, the hôtel which has become a hotel – arguably *the* hotel. Founded by César Ritz in 1898, the Paris Ritz has given its name to a whole style of life, characterized by luxury and glamour. The word alone conjures images of film stars, celebrities and wealthy aristocrats. Its patrons have ranged from Somerset Maugham to Marlene Dietrich. Marcel Proust once remarked that what he liked most about the Ritz was that it observed with great seriousness 'the first and noblest rule of hotels: discretion'.

On the other side of the square, among the even numbers, a plaque to Chopin outside number 12 marks the house where he died on 17 October 1849. At number 16, where the Bank of India now has offices, Dr Mesmer established his clinic for nervous illnesses in 1778. His system was based on harnessing 'animal magnetism' by seating patients round a large tub from which projected metal strips used to transmit the vital fluid. It enjoyed undreamed-of success. The rich and poor of Paris crowded to his door, swelling the doctor's revenues and overrunning the Hôtel Moufle. In the end a government commission set up to investigate his miraculous cures pronounced them to be little more than a confidence trick, but by that time Mesmer had sold his secret for 340,000 livres to the Freemasons and could make a comfortable retreat to England.

At number 26, where Boucheron now displays its exquisite pieces of jewellery, lived "the madwoman of the place Vendôme', the Comtesse de Castiglione. She came here in 1878, hung the walls with black, veiled all the mirrors to avoid being confronted by the ravages of old age, and went out only by night, through a side entrance specially constructed for her. Inside her apartment the blinds were always drawn and the bed was covered with sheets of black silk. After sixteen years she moved to the rue Cambon, where she died.

The column which rises in the centre of the square was Napoleon's idea, though, to be fair, the imperial statue of him on top was not. Spiralling round the

Napoleon in the guise of a Roman Emperor at the top of the column in the place Vendôme. Napoleon's interest in antiquity led him to bring back to Paris vast numbers of antique statues from Italy and Egypt.

column are bronze bas-reliefs honouring the victors of the Battle of Austerlitz. (The details are easier to make out on the model displayed in the Musée de l'Armée (pp. 87–8.) In a country given to revolutions, public monuments tend to lead a precarious existence. When the Commune took over Paris in 1871, the Vendôme column came crashing to the ground in an act of vandalism directed by the painter Gustave Courbet. It was an unlucky day's work for Courbet. After the suppression of the Commune he was obliged to restore the column to its place at his own expense. The cost ruined him.

Close at hand for the favourites of Society was Society's favourite church. Begun in 1764, the ÉGLISE DE LA MADELEINE looks like a suitable edifice for a national museum or a particularly pompous bank (which is what at one stage it nearly became). Though it ended up as a church, consecrated in 1842 after a spell as a Temple de la Gloire in the early years of the century, it is not altogether easy to imagine people going in there to worship anything this side of the classical gods and godesses. The Madeleine has, however, done useful service for society weddings and funerals, including the funeral of Chopin. Moreover, it enjoys a spectacular situation. From the flight of steps in front of it the eye is drawn along one of the great vistas in this part of Paris: down the rue Royale to the place de la Concorde, and beyond it to the Palais Bourbon and the Invalides.

The Madeleine's rather lifeless dignity is offset by a rich display of flowers in the neighbouring market and an almost equally absorbing array of foodstuffs in the windows of Fauchon, a sort of Parisian Fortnum and Mason which caters in appropriate style for the material needs of the Madeleine's parishioners.

Leading away from the church, the rue Royale has the look of a street that was designed for processions. Wedding parties and funeral cortèges were only one facet of this; it was also along the rue Royale that the tumbrils rolled towards the guillotine in the place de la Concorde. Today it is lined with the expensive shops that are a feature of the area. Just before we reach the bottom, we pass the unostentatious entrance to Maxim's. Like so many good things, it was a product of the 1890s, and it preserves the art nouveau decor of the period. Within a few years it had won popularity among an exotic mixture of the international nobility and the upper reaches of the Parisian demi-monde. Think of the *belle époque* and thoughts of Maxim's will not be far behind.

Standing by its doorway, we are already on the edge of Paris's most majestic square, which was laid out in the eighteenth century under Louis XV. In a perfect world the place de la Concorde would be forbidden ground to cars, vans, lorries, mopeds and fast-moving bicycles, but for the moment those wishing to see the obelisk at close quarters must either walk round to the crossing-point or nerve themselves for the death-run across a wide expanse of road entirely at the mercy of French motorists out to bag slow-footed pedestrians. If the railing around the obelisk chances to be open, you can then position yourself for a particularly satisfying view up the Champs-Elysées. Dusk is the time I prefer, ideally the twilight of a summer evening, when the lights along the Champs challenge a fading glow that spreads from the sky behind the Arc de Triomphe.

The obelisk comes from the same temple in Luxor as Cleopatra's Needle on the Thames embankment and dates from the time of Rameses II, the Pharaoh from whom the Children of Israel escaped under the leadership of Moses. Both of these colossal monuments were sent to Europe by the Viceroy of Egypt, who was attempting to curry favour with the European monarchs. In the case of France this was a long-term business, since the obelisk took four years to get to its destination. By the time it reached the capital in 1833, Charles X, to whom it had been sent, was already dead. An inscription at the base tells us that it was erected on its pedestal by the engineer M. Lebas to the acclamation of a massive crowd on 25 October 1836. Complex, and to me quite incomprehensible, diagrams, also on the base, explain how it was transported. Anyone who wants to know the story might do better to begin with the narrative in the Maritime Museum.

One of the great virtues of an obelisk is its lofty neutrality. Unlike statues of kings, emperors and statesmen, it incites no one to pull it down when the political climate changes. For that reason alone it would be an ideal monument for the centre of Paris; but placed as it is in the middle of the splendid prospect from the Arc de Triomphe to the Louvre, it has a commanding presence which quite outstrips that of its cousin beside the Thames.

Political neutrality is not something that came early to the place de la Concorde. Initially its centre-piece was an unpopular statue of Louis XV, which was duly demolished in 1792 to be replaced by a huge statue representing Liberty. But Liberty was an even more relative concept than usual during the Revolution and before long the statue had a companion piece in the shape of the guillotine. 'Liberty! Liberty! what crimes are committed in thy name,' said Mme Roland, looking at the statue as she set her foot to the scaffold. In the course of three bloody years 1119 people were executed here – the place de la Révolution, as it was then called. Among the victims were some of the most eminent architects of the Revolution as well as its most notable enemies: Danton and Robespierre died here, as did Louis XVI, Marie-Antoinette and Charlotte Corday.

Around the edge of the square are eight pavilions surmounted by statues representing France's principal cities. You might reasonably feel that life is too short to give much time to these, but Pradier's statue of Strasbourg, opposite Lille at the north-east corner, has a subsidiary interest in that its model was Juliette Drouet, the long-serving, long-suffering mistress of Victor Hugo. (She would have every right to feel that the sulky battle-axe Pradier has created does her less than justice.) For almost 50 years, until the end of World War I, this statue was hung with black, Strasbourg having been taken over by Germany after the Franco-Prussian war.

Not far from here people emerge in a continual stream from the Concorde Métro stop. It was the scene in this station that prompted Ezra Pound to compose the most famous of Imagist poems, 'In a Station of the Metro':

The apparition of these faces in the crowd;
petals on a wet, black bough.

From our vantage point beside the obelisk we can glance back up the rue Royale towards the Madeleine, which actually looks rather better at this distance. We can also get a clearer view of the two buildings between which we entered the square, on one side the Hôtel Crillon, on the other the Hôtel de la Marine, now the headquarters of the navy. It was at the Crillon that Benjamin Franklin, among others, signed the Treaty of Friendship and Trade between France and America with Louis XVI. Appropriately enough, the American Embassy now stands just opposite, on the other side of the rue Boissy d'Anglas. In 1944 the Hôtel Crillon was the scene of fierce fighting at the end of the German Occupation.

At the south-east corner of the square, beside the Tuileries, is a museum not to be missed. In the days when the neighbouring Jeu de Paume housed the main collection of French Impressionists, the ORANGERIE tended to be noticed chiefly for its temporary exhibitions, but since then it has come into its own. It is an airy gallery with plenty of light which holds a memorable collection of early twentieth-century paintings. Matisse, Renoir, Derain, Utrillo and Douanier Rousseau are all represented. Among its many attractions are Rousseau's doom-laden picture *La Noce* and Marie Laurencin's wistful portrait from 1923 of Mlle Chanel. Downstairs are Monet's *Les Nymphées*, the eight huge paintings inspired by his garden at Giverny, which he offered to the nation *'comme un bouquet de fleurs'*. He supervised their arrangement in the Orangerie, but with the provision that they should not be shown to the public until after his death – perhaps because in a curious way these almost abstract paintings were too personal.

The pont de la Concorde has nothing special to offer the sightseer in the way of structure or view – it leads straight towards the Palais Bourbon, seat of the Assemblée Nationale – but it does have one uncommon feature to recommend it. Since it was being built at the time that the Bastille was demolished, stones from the old fortress were brought here to be used for the upper part of its piers. This was a satisfactory arrangement for reasons both of economy and of symbolism. The ardent revolutionary could now feel that the stones of tyranny were being trampled underfoot forever.

We enter the Champs-Elysées past two celebrated eighteenth-century statues of rearing horses, the *'chevaux de Marly'*. Like the bronze horses of San Marco in Venice, the originals have now been retired to a display room, safe from the corrosive air which the rest of us continue to breathe. Their tough new replicas have been designed to last well into the next millennium. The prospect that stretches ahead of us as we walk past them is at the heart of Paris's mythology, an image that encapsulates its claims to history, vision, fashion and glamour. By the time we have gasped our way up to the Arc de Triomphe, the image is likely to have taken something of a battering. To trudge past rows of fast food outlets, car show rooms, airline offices and ugly cinemas inevitably taxes one's sense of romance; but then by some odd chemistry one wakes up the next morning to find the lustrous image of the Champs-Elysées splendidly intact again, quite untroubled by this brush with reality.

OPPOSITE *Pradier's statue of Strasbourg seated at the corner of the place de la Concorde.*

From the place de la Concorde we begin with the wooded section which leads towards the Rond Point and which still gives a faint hint of the origins of the street's name. Until well after the Napoleonic wars, at the end of which encampments of English and Russian troops did what they could to make a wasteland of the area, the whole district was undeveloped. Apart from half-a-dozen private mansions, the scene was wooded countryside, frequented for the most part by footpads, but occasionally by less predictable elements. In November 1788 a member of the watch noted in his report:

> Arrested, towards 8 in the evening, a clergyman with a negress. Alleged that he
> was her confessor and was giving her instruction. Released with a caution not to
> be found again confessing his penitents under the trees, by night.

It was only during the mid nineteenth century that the Champs, illuminated now by an array of gas-lamps and furnished with cafés, restaurants and theatres, began to acquire the status of the capital's main pleasure gardens. Streets like the avenue Montaigne, which are today given over to the sober life of well-heeled residents, expensive couturiers and members of a few discreet, highly paid professions, were then notorious for the unbridled hedonism of the public dancing that was their chief attraction.

At the edge of the place Clemenceau, surrounded by trees, are the Petit Palais and the Grand Palais, built for the Exhibition of 1900. The PETIT PALAIS is now the home of the MUSÉE DES BEAUX-ARTS DE LA VILLE DE PARIS. It has the merit of being half empty most of the time, but this is not altogether without reason. Many of its paintings are undistinguished, and some, like Bouguereau's *Virgin among the Angels*, are truly ghastly. On the credit side, there are some lovely Flemish paintings and a number of interesting works by the Impressionists. The seventeenth- and eighteenth-century galleries have a display of good furniture, including a sedan chair in beautifully sculpted and gilded wood, made for the niece of Louis XIV.

On the other side of the road, the GRAND PALAIS has in recent years been used primarily for mounting large exhibitions.

At some stage the long walk up the populous second half of the Champs is indispensable, but for the moment, on the assumption that this is a sunny weekend, we shall cross from the Grand Palais to observe the curiosities of the Paris stamp market, which sets out its stalls along the south side of the avenue Gabriel, at the edge of the wooded area. Things rarely have the dramatic excitement of the scene at the climax of Stanley Donen's film *Charade*, but whether philately holds any charm for you or not, there is a fascination in the sheer quantity, colour and range of subject matter of the endless sheets of stamps produced anywhere from Andorra to Antarctica. Those, like myself, who know little about it can derive simple pleasure from merely browsing through the different designs, all neatly catalogued, from cats to cars, butterflies to circus acts. Behind the stalls enthusiasts sit on folding chairs, surrounded by a battery of files and reference books, ready to do business.

Close to the stamp market is the British Embassy, which was formerly the home of Napoleon's sister, Pauline Bonaparte. To reach the entrance of this imposing eighteenth-century hôtel we shall have to walk round to the rue du Faubourg-Saint-Honoré. In the course of the nineteenth century the embassy was the scene of the marriage of Berlioz and later of Thackeray, of readings by Dickens, of the birth of Somerset Maugham and of a string of glittering social events; but we can get little nearer to such echoes from the past, since its rooms are closed to the public.

On our way to the embassy we shall pass the heavily guarded gates of the Elysée Palace, once the property of Madame de Pompadour and now the official residence of the French President. This also is closed to the public. Not that anyone in their right mind really comes to the rue du Faubourg-Saint-Honoré to peer through the gates of the British Embassy or the Elysée Palace. The envious looks take a quite different direction. This is where you come to press your face against the windows of the world's most fashionable and expensive shops. Between here and the rue Royale the devotee will find such names as Hermès and Laroche, Lagerfeld and Lancôme, Aramis, Courrèges and Saint-Laurent. The bitter-sweet pleasures of window shopping are nowhere more seductive.

Having gazed our fill on the imaginative clothes and even more imaginative prices, we can turn north to the boulevard Haussmann, named after the man who did more than anyone else to shape Paris into the city we know today. Baron Georges Eugène Haussmann was Prefect of the Seine under Napoleon III and not a man much given to self-questioning. Faced with a city that still bore many of the hallmarks of the Middle Ages, he acted with ruthless decision to enforce his programme of modernization. Through the 1850s and 1860s he tore down street after street of the dark, cramped, picturesque buildings which had characterized the old Paris and set in their place the wide boulevards and dignified architecture that we associate with the Second Empire. For better or worse, and it was not always worse, he left his mark upon every quarter of the city.

The atmosphere of the boulevard Haussmann is respectable, moneyed, a bit dull. This is not an area in which one's walk is likely to produce many surprises. Close to the Métro station of Saint-Augustin a plaque at number 102 indicates the building, now occupied by a bank, where Marcel Proust lived from 1907 to 1919, while he worked on his immense novel *Á la recherche du temps perdu* in a room specially lined with cork to keep it insulated from the noise of the street. Perhaps the best reason for making one's way up to this boulevard is not to pay tribute either to Haussmann or to Proust but to visit the MUSÉE JACQUEMART-ANDRÉ, set back from the street behind a railed wall at number 158. Run by the Institut de France, it has an important range of eighteenth-century French art as well as some fine Italian pieces from the Renaissance, including paintings by Mantegna and Uccello.

From this part of the boulevard Haussmann it is only a short distance to the PARC MONCEAU. At the time when Proust lived nearby, its clientèle was largely made up of the children of the well-to-do and their neatly uniformed *bonnes*. Even

The Parc Monceau is relatively unknown by visitors and even at the height of summer remains peaceful.

in these more democratic times the wealth of the surrounding 8th arrondissement makes its presence strongly felt along the paths that wind among the park's well tended lawns and curious follies. Laid out in the reign of Louis XVI, the Parc Monceau was originally sprinkled with all manner of kiosks, pavilions, pagodas, temples, pyramids, mills, rivers and 'antique' ruins. Most of these have gone, some of them destroyed by the construction of the Farmers General Wall along the line of the boulevard de Courcelles, others by the later building programmes of the 1850s. But the few that have survived – fluted columns, crumbling pyramids and broken archways, folded in among the cunning undulations of the ground – make this of all the Paris parks my favourite. One of the toll gates of the old tax wall stands at the entrance just beside the Métro – a rotunda that is now known as the Pavillon de Chartres.

Overlooking the Parc Monceau are two museums that invite our attention. The first, perhaps of more specialist interest, is the MUSÉE CERNUSCHI. It displays the collection of Henri Cernuschi, a Milanese who travelled in Japan in the 1870s and then built this house as a setting for the works of art he had acquired there. It was the period just after the Meiji restoration, and the temples in Japan sold him a number of valuable pieces, including a colossal Buddha from Meguro in Tokyo. Among the Chinese art exhibited here is a beautiful seventeenth-century screen and a couple of poignant fragments of T'ang mural painting.

The second museum, which for me ranks as one of the loveliest in Paris, is the MUSÉE NISSIM DE CAMONDO. Talleyrand once remarked that those who had not lived before the Revolution had never kown '*la vraie douceur de vivre*'. In the Musée Nissim de Camondo the *douceur de vivre* of eighteenth-century Paris is laid before us in room after room of sumptuous furniture. Tables, chairs, carpets, tapestries, plates, ornaments, paintings, even the exquisite library steps – all were produced in the four or five precious decades immediately before the Revolution. The quiet rooms, disturbed by no more than an occasional visitor, look down to a trim garden backing on to the Parc Monceau, and as you survey their beautiful furnishings you have the sense that for once they are not objects in a museum but part of a way of life. The Revolution that brought it to an end was only one holocaust among many. A notice at the entrance tells us that the museum was created in memory of a son killed in an air combat in 1917. Underneath, another plaque indicates that the last representatives of the family who once lived among so many rare and beautiful objects were deported during World War II and died at Auschwitz leaving no descendants.

From the western end of the Parc Monceau we can stroll down the broad avenue Hoche to finish our walk at the place de l'Étoile. For some years now this has officially been called the place Charles-de-Gaulle, but Parisians have sensibly refused to take much notice of this, preferring to stick with the apt and evocative name which the *place* had enjoyed for the previous hundred years. Dominating this unparalleled site is the ARC DE TRIOMPHE, erected over the first thirty years of the nineteenth century. It is superb, of course, but I cannot help regretting that Louis XV's engineer was not allowed to get his way. His sublime vision was to crown the site with a gigantic elephant. A due sense of tact led him to propose a statue of the king on top of it, but this would no doubt have been dispensed with by the Revolution and we should now look up from the place de la Concorde towards a splendid lone elephant.

As things are, we must take the Arc for what it is, a handsome piece of national self-glorification. As a symbol of France's greatness it has been at best an ambiguous success. In the last century the victorious Prussians marched through it and in this century the image that obstinately recurs to many people's minds is that of the victorious Germans marching through it. It would perhaps be ungenerous to remark on this if the arch itself were not such an irritatingly complacent piece of work, with its pompous record of national victories – no mention of any defeat – and its punctilious register of the names of 558 army generals, balancing the anonymity of most of those who were actually getting killed. Still, it is, in its way, an impressive affair, and if we look at it from the Champs-Elysées we can see on the right of the arch François Rude's admirable depiction of the Departure of the Volunteers in 1792 (also known as La Marseillaise). This is a spirited, almost nightmarish piece of work, which strikes a resonant note of horror into the

Looking south from the Arc de Triomphe to the 16th arrondissement under a louring sky.

general atmosphere of pious celebration. Beneath the arch the flame has burned in tribute to the unknown soldier since 1923.

Over the past few years, the view from the platform of the Arc de Triomphe has changed less to the east than it has to the west. Beyond the avenue de la Grande-Armée there now rise the cluster of towers that mark La Défense, bounded by the giant arch which faces the Arc de Triomphe – a structure so huge that its interior space could contain the whole of Notre-Dame, including the spire. This new complex of skyscrapers is probably the sort of thing that many tourists have gone on holiday to get away from, but if time allows, you should certainly make the short trip by RER to have a closer look at it.

After a rocky start, LA DÉFENSE is beginning to mature. It is still slightly disquieting to emerge from underground into a world that looks like the set for an early science fiction film, but already the lines of the place are beginning to soften as the trees and shrubs grow up. And the skyscrapers, among them the tall black Fiat tower and the Manhattan tower with its rippling colours, have a bleak sort of individuality. The area is arranged as a series of terraces – vast open patios with fountains, cafés and sculptures – lined by these vaguely threatening giants. Despite the inhuman scale of the place, there is, as usual in Paris, a feeling that trouble has been taken to make it as agreeable as possible. A small gallery displays models of the buildings and projected buildings, with a map that lights up to show the location of various pieces of sculpture, among which are works by Joan Mirò and Alexander Calder.

By chance, I happened to see La Défense for the first time just after I had returned from a visit to Versailles, and it seemed to me then not altogether absurd to think that it might in time look as impressive an achievement for the twentieth century as that monstrous palace was for the seventeenth. It has the confidence of a city that sees itself as the capital of a new Europe. Looking at it in the evening sunlight, one has a sense that after all the future might just about work.

OPPOSITE *Does Paris offer a glimpse of the future in the architecture of La Défense?*

3
The West

······························

Even in an age as fanatically dedicated to tourism as our own, visiting sewers remains only moderately popular. For my part, I can take it or leave it and would on the whole prefer to leave it. Nevertheless, the Paris sewers do have a certain pungent interest, so the really serious sightseer will sometimes be found stepping nervously underground at the corner of the pont de l'Alma and the quai d'Orsay. A spiral staircase leads down into the network of passageways which, as a notice informs us, add up to some 2100 kilometres, the distance from Paris to Istanbul. The well-designed tour takes us past rivers of grey-green water into a long gallery with a bust of the engineer Eugène Belgrand and a series of explanatory displays. The smell, mainly but not entirely chemical, means that only enthusiasts are likely to take in very much of the explanation. (My own pathetic eagerness to be away caused me on a recent visit to drop my pen in a fumble of haste. With poetic justice it slid neatly through the grating to join the tide flowing beneath me – an inoffensive contribution to the 15,000 cubic feet of solid waste drawn from the system each year.) At the souvenir stall near the exit you can buy key-rings, biros and pocket calculators, all containing water from the Paris sewers, as well as model rats and copies of Hugo's *Les Misérables*. Alongside the souvenirs, an ornate fountain dispenses drinking water, but I saw no one try it. A silent slide show completes the tour.

At the end of this invigorating trip, you may not feel much inclined to linger in the area, but have a quick look at the lone statue under the northern end of the pont de l'Alma: a noble zouave with a long rifle beside him, looking out towards the far bank. He is the survivor of a group of four soldiers that decorated the previous bridge, and he now serves to indicate the water-level of the Seine.

For those who want a change of scene, the pont de l'Alma is a convenient place from which to take the RER out to VERSAILLES. Sooner or later it has to be done, although more than once I have found myself putting it off until the next day. The best advice is to go when you are feeling sociable – the park and palace

OPPOSITE *A tranquil view of the 680-metre-long garden front of the palace of Versailles in the early evening.*

69

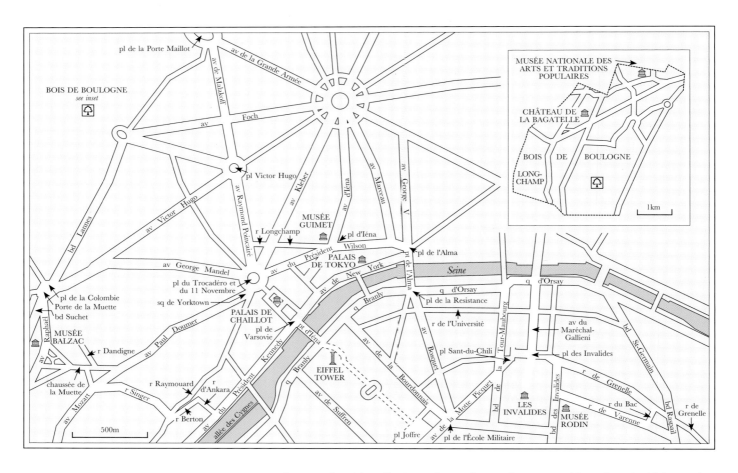

THE WEST

are thronged with pilgrims throughout the year. For the dutiful tourist, Versailles, like the Parthenon or the pyramids, is inescapable. Unlike them, however, it bears the characteristic stamp of one individual. The myth of Apollo, which pervades the decorative scheme of the palace, is at the heart of the whole enterprise. The Sun God – fit symbol for *le Roi Soleil* – reappears in different guises at every turn, proclaiming the semi-divine status of the château's creator. Versailles is the physical embodiment of Louis XIV's concept of his own majesty, and it will leave you either stunned by its grandeur or revolted by its self-aggrandisement.

The rationale for spending something over 60,000,000 livres was summed up by Colbert, Louis's superintendent of finances, when he remarked that buildings came next after battles as a way of augmenting a king's prestige. That architecture could be a political statement was something Louis had already learned. When Nicolas Fouquet, Colbert's predecessor, had invited the young king to his superb new château of Vaux-le-Vicomte near Melun, Louis was quick to take in all that it implied about the wealth and status of his minister. Unfortunately for Fouquet, the statement was in this case rather too persuasive. The grandeur of the château and its gardens left Louis feeling jealous and belittled. Before long Fouquet had exchanged Vaux-le-Vicomte for the prison of the Arsénal and Louis was contemplating schemes of his own. To make sure that there would be no mistake, he commandeered the trio who had been responsible for the beauties of Vaux-le-Vicomte and set them to work on Versailles: Louis Le Vau was to design the palace, Charles Le Brun to decorate the interior and André Le Nôtre to lay out the gardens.

Plans for the new château got underway in 1661, and for the next 50 years Versailles was the scene of more or less constant building. Le Vau himself died in 1670 and was succeeded for a time by one of his pupils, but in the later years of the century it was Jules Hardouin-Mansart, appointed chief architect in 1678, who left his mark most decisively on Versailles. He was responsible for reworking the old château built by Louis XIII and also for modifying the newer buildings that had already been created around it.

Whether you opt for a guided tour or set out on your own, you will see only a fraction of the palace in a single visit; and that will probably be quite enough. The frustrations of trying to catch the words of your guide across a sea of heads are matched by the annoyance of being jostled aside by impatient groups if you try to linger for more than a few moments over a scene by Boucher or a Gobelins tapestry. Few people, surely, can emerge from the château wishing their visit had been longer. The rooms stretch ahead of one in a relentless succession, decorated with busts, battle-scenes, portraits and allegories, almost all of them tending one way or another to reinforce the overriding message of the glory of the Bourbon dynasty and of Louis XIV in particular.

For the visitor who is avid of historical sites, here are the rooms where Louis XIV was laid out after his death, where Louis XVI was born, where Mme de Pompadour died, where Mozart played before the ladies of the court in 1763, where Molière's *Tartuffe* was first performed, where members of the queen's bodyguard were cut down by the mob in October 1789. It was in Mansart's magnificent *Galerie des Glaces*, with its ceiling by Le Brun and its seven huge mirrors facing the seven windows, that the Treaty of Versailles was signed on 28 June 1919 after World War I. Today the great gallery looks in need of refurbishment, but the effect is still impressive – even more so if we think of the enormous cost of mirror glass in the seventeenth century when it had to be specially imported from Venice.

Impressive in a different way is the elaborate chapel, decorated in white and gold, which was begun by Mansart and finished in 1710 by Robert de Cotte. That it was completed at all is remarkable enough, given the state of the country's finances at the time. On the whole, the fortunes of Versailles fluctuated with the alternation of war and peace throughout Louis XIV's reign. When France was at peace, money was poured with crippling prodigality into the various projects connected with the château, but in times of war the resources were sharply curtailed. The chapel was one exception to this rule. At a time when France's military fortunes were at their lowest ebb, its army reeling under the onslaughts of the

Duke of Marlborough, the ageing and increasingly pious king insisted on pushing the chapel through to its completion, regardless, for once, of the opposition of Mme de Maintenon.

Françoise de Maintenon was one of several royal mistresses who played a part in the development of Versailles. Apart from her sobering, not to say dampening, influence on the life of the court, she also inspired Louis to create the Grand Trianon in 1687. This miniature palace was intended to serve as a refuge from the constraints of life at the château. The need to escape was part of the price Louis paid for bringing the court to Versailles, where his palace became the theatre for a grotesquely elaborate system of etiquette. Bounded by the ceremonies of the *lever* and the *coucher*, this rigid code of precedence, with its endlessly trivial ramifications, was used to absorb the energies of the courtiers Louis had drawn into his gorgeous web. It was crucial to his design that the nobility should remain effectively pinned down in Versailles, but to achieve this he had himself to become a prisoner of the rituals that held them there. The Trianon offered at least a temporary retreat.

In the following century Louis XV indulged in a similar truancy when he created the Petit Trianon for Mme de Pompadour. She died before the building was completed and it passed to her successor Mme du Barry. Later it was to provide the scene for Marie-Antoinette's pastoral fantasies. The thatched cottages beside the *Grand Lac* are survivors of the hamlet designed for her by Mique to offer a sanitized version of rural life, a place where she and her friends could indulge themselves in a make-believe return to the Golden Age. In the diary, equipped with marble walls and flooring, the queen, prettily dressed for the part, visited the cows and churned the butter, careless of the storm-clouds of revolution that were gathering beyond the confines of her enchanted park.

From the start it was recognized that this park was to be one of the glories of Versailles, and its creator, André Le Nôtre, was accorded a corresponding status. An honest and straightforward man in a world of courtiers, he lived through the whole process that gave birth to Versailles, managing somehow to retain the favour, and even the affection, of the king. His formal gardens, geometrically arranged and sprinkled with statuary, are the apotheosis of the French manner. Extending across 250 acres, they are still a spectacular sight, but to appreciate them fully, you need to choose one of the Sundays in summer when the lavishly sculpted fountains are allowed to play. From here, looking back towards the façade of the palace (all 680 metres of it), you can get some sense of the sheer scale of Louis's enterprise. It is an awesome achievement, although not perhaps an altogether attractive one. The 30,000 men who laboured to create it have produced something unequalled in its kind, but whether the result of their labours was a marvel or a monster is less easy to determine.

Back at the pont de l'Alma we have an afternoon of museums ahead of us. The prospect sounds daunting, but on the whole the least crowded museums tend also to be the least tiring, and many of those we shall be visiting will leave us untroubled by fellow-tourists. From the bridge with its solitary zouave the unin-

OPPOSITE *Four different marbles are used in Mansart's circular colonnade, built between 1685 and 1688, in the southern groves of the park at Versailles.*

spiring avenue du Président-Wilson takes us towards the place d'Iéna, where we shall find the entrance to the PALAIS DE TOKYO.

Built for the World Exhibition of 1937, this is now the home of the MUSÉE D'ART MODERNE DE LA VILLE DE PARIS. Since the opening of the Pompidou Centre its attractions have been much depleted, but it still contains an interesting range of canvasses, including works by Matisse, Bonnard, Modigliani, Derain, Rouault, Foujita and Chagall. The museum is light and blissfully empty, but it is also slightly eerie. Intended for more people, it has the sense of a place that, in spite of a number of impeccably avant-garde exhibits, has been left behind. One of its most endearing pieces is the monster painting by Raoul Dufy, *La Fée Electricité*, which has a room to itself and measures 10 metres by 60. It is not one of his best paintings, but it is certainly his biggest. Painted at the behest of the Parisian electricity company for the 1937 Exhibition, it has two hundred and fifty panels, which together make it the largest painting in the world.

Museums are too thick on the ground hereabouts for anyone but a super-tourist to do them justice. If time is short or your stamina is running low, abandon all the rest and head for the MUSÉE GUIMET. This beautifully laid-out museum of oriental art is a joy to visit. Arranged by geographical area, it is so well-lit and well-organized that for once you may find yourself almost sad that it is as empty as it probably will be. To do justice to its treasures would require a separate volume rather than a couple of lines. Whether you turn to the twelfth-century Khmer elephant, 'upholder of the world', from Angkor Wat, or the eighteenth-century Chinese screen, all twelve leaves of it, with its brilliant display of birds and flowers on a gilt background, or the delicate Japanese illustrations of *The Tale of Genji* from the same period, you will find exhibits that make the Musée Guimet a place of pilgrimage for anyone with the faintest enthusiasm for oriental art.

We are not done with museums yet, for at the end of the avenue du Président-Wilson is another monumental – and monumentally ugly – building constructed for the 1937 Exhibition, the PALAIS DE CHAILLOT. Whatever one thinks of the building itself, its forecourt commands a splendid view across the Seine to the Eiffel Tower. This used to be the playground of Paris's skaters. One figure now sadly absent is the shabby, upright old man who used to haunt this place until the mid 1970s. In a worn grey suit he would arrive here on Sunday afternoons carrying a wind-up gramophone, set it down at the corner of the top level near one of the gilded statues, and then amid the tumbling children skate serenely round this open terrace, wrapped in a dream of other times.

Skaters are still to be seen, but they have been largely displaced by skateboarders, and these in turn give way during the summer to the ubiquitous sellers of North African goods, who spread out their belts, bangles, purses and bags on a cloth and then wait for the tourists. All seem to sell identical wares, and their prices are geared to whatever the volatile market will bear. A move to walk away can reduce a bracelet from 200 francs to 20 in as little time as it takes to say it.

Before turning back to the palace to confront its array of museums, we might stroll for a moment in the pleasant gardens that slope away to the right and left of

OPPOSITE *The Eiffel Tower framed by the fountains of the Palais de Chaillot.*

the terraces. On the left hand side, in front of the children's playground, steps lead down to the rusting entrance of the old aquarium, which sticks in my mind as the only place where I have ever seen a specimen of the extraordinary Mexican amphibian called the axolotl. I had dodged in here one wet afternoon to escape the weather and suddenly found myself being stared at by one of these creatures, with its grotesque face, like a distorted baby's, pressed up against the glass of the tank. I passed quickly on, preferring the rain. For years now there has been talk of reopening the aquarium, but it looks more closed than ever.

The museums are all entered from the side of the palace that faces on to the place du Trocadéro, so we must walk back between the two wings and then take our pick from the Musée de la Marine, the Musée de l'Homme, the Musée du Cinéma and the Musée des Monuments Français. If we take the west wing first, on the right, we shall find ourselves at the entrance of the Musée de la Marine and Musée de l'Homme. The names of both museums strike something of a chill, but do not be put off. Apart from some fine models, that range from seventeenth-century men-of-war to modern oil tankers, the MUSÉE DE LA MARINE (Maritime Museum) has an intriguingly diverse collection of exhibits. In a way it is the fragmentary items from the past – the odd spars, anchors, bits of rope, broken pieces of cannon – that give the most striking idea of the heroic scale of early sea-faring. Mighty figureheads taken from the prows of ships long ago destroyed lean into the exhibition rooms, dwarfing the spectator. Elsewhere, an interesting display gives details of the transport of the obelisk in the place de la Concorde from Luxor (p. 57). In order to get it stowed, the bows of the ship had to be completely sawn off and afterwards replaced.

Just opposite this exhibit is one of the museum's most recent acquisitions, a Vietnamese fishing boat which actually made the hazardous journey to Songkla in southern Thailand, carrying fourteen boat-people to precarious safety in the summer of 1987. With its two guardian eyes painted on the bow and the rusty nails sticking casually out of its worn planks, it gives a more vivid impression of what the journeys of the boat-people mean in reality than any number of news stories and documentary reports on the television.

At the other extreme of our unequal world, you might note, before you leave, the imperial barge built for Napoleon in a staggering 21 days in 1810.

The MUSÉE DE L'HOMME (Museum of Mankind) is in its way equally fascinating. In contrast to most of Paris's museums, it has a slightly old-fashioned feel to it, but renovations are in progress at the moment. Its range of exhibits is huge. If you want to study anything from the instruments of the Indonesian Gamelan to the layout of a Hopi village at the end of the nineteenth century, this is the place to come. Among the items that might catch your eye are a colossal head from Easter Island, some striking masks from the Pacific – especially a hook-nosed character from New Caledonia – a model of the mythical creature from Bali called the Barong, wedding costumes from the Celebes, Samurai armour, a display of photographs taken by travellers to Tibet at the turn of the century, tableaux of Inuit life, a Hungarian shepherd's hut, a model of a Senegalese village and the costume for an Angolan circumcision dance. If at least one of these does not excite your curiosity, then you can probably afford to give the Musée de l'Homme a miss.

The two museums in the east wing of the Palais de Chaillot are notably different from each other. Downstairs is the MUSÉE DU CINÉMA, where a model of the Gaumont Palace greets you in the entrance hall. From 1931 to 1972 this stood in the place de Clichy and had the distinction of being the largest cinema in the world. The museum is a treat for cinema-lovers, but be warned, it is not a French version of the Universal Studios tour. A lot of the information is fairly technical, and since admission is only by guided tour you need to speak French to make much sense of it. The museum opens out into room after room of posters, photographs, historical displays, cinematic apparatus from the past and relics from celebrated films. Both guide and audience are likely to be enthusiasts, so progress is often slow and you should allow a couple of hours for the visit.

On the upper floors of the same building, the MUSÉE DES MONUMENTS FRANÇAIS deserves to be more visited than it is. Its relative unpopularity is due to the fact that it is a museum of copies rather than originals. Inspired by Viollet-le-Duc in the nineteenth century, it now displays carefully worked reproductions of sculpture and architecture from all over France. It is obviously not the same as seeing the pieces in their rightful setting, but to have looked in detail at the copy of Robert Le Lorrain's *Horses of Apollo* adds rather than detracts from the experience of coming upon the real thing at some later stage in the courtyard of the Hôtel de Rohan (p. 152). Or take the figures of Claude de France and François I from Saint-Denis (pp. 169–71). Sadly, it is almost impossible for visitors to the cathedral to get a proper view of the originals, but to have seen them here is some compensation. Claude de France, in particular, with her long, delicate fingers, and her sunken breasts, her hair swept back and lips slightly parted, offers a moving image of death.

After this spate of museums, a few hours' relaxation would probably be welcome. Unless your tastes run to the dangerously *louche*, the BOIS DE BOULOGNE is not a place to head for once dusk has started to fall, but on a summer afternoon, with cultural duties done, we are well placed to sample its pleasures. The Bois is poorly served by the Métro, so our easiest means of approach is either by taxi or by the bus which leaves from near the Porte Maillot Métro station.

The remnant of a huge forest which covered the area in prehistoric times, the Bois de Boulogne was for long a wild region used as a refuge for criminals and a hunting ground for the nobility. In the course of the seventeenth and eighteenth centuries it became increasingly fashionable among the aristocracy as a place for duels, debauchery and social excursions. It was during this period that a number of its great landmarks came into being: the Folie Saint-James, the châteaux of Bagatelle, La Muette and Madrid, the allée de Longchamp and so on. The Revolution, as usual, brought destruction, and a few years later the encampment here of the British and Russian armies brought further destruction. Again it was Haussmann who took the place in hand, giving it more or less the appearance it

RIGHT *The grounds of the Château de la Bagatelle boast a rose-garden, an expensive restaurant in the old stable-block and a garden filled with 'English' flowers and shrubs.*

OPPOSITE *A charming place for a rendez-vous in the Bois de Boulogne, the Château de la Bagatelle was built in 1777 for the Comte d'Artois, later Charles X. During the Revolution, it was used as a tavern.*

has today and turning it back into a fashionable resort of the *beau monde*, frequented by the sort of figures whose lives are chronicled by Marcel Proust.

Unless we have come here for the racing at LONGCHAMP – the Prix de l'Arc de Triomphe is run in early October – we shall probably want to do no more than stroll around the extensive park, taking in whatever sights come our way. For an agreeable picnic, we might follow the eastern edge of the Lac Inférieur and take the ferry across to the island, where the sort of businessmen whose expense accounts can stand the bill will just be settling down to lunch at the attractive restaurant. If we walk past them and over the bridge, we should be able to find, on the smaller of the two islands, a shaded spot overlooking the lake.

Without a bicycle – and they can only be rented for an exorbitant fee – most people are unlikely to take in more than one or two of the attractions of the Bois on a single visit. Among the places of interest, it is worth bearing in mind the unusual Shakespeare Garden in which all the trees and flowers are named in Shakespeare's plays. There is also the Grande Cascade, as well as the Pré Catelan, which according to the legend acquired its name when the trouba-

dour Arnould de Catelan was murdered here at the beginning of the fourteenth century on his way to the court of Philippe le Bel. But if time is limited, my choice would be for the CHÂTEAU DE LA BAGATELLE. Incredibly, it was built in 64 days in 1777 by the Comte d'Artois, younger brother of Louis XVI, for a wager with Marie-Antoinette. Nine hundred workers were set on the job day and night, and patrols of Swiss Guards swept the neighbourhood, commandeering any building materials they could find. The result was an exquisite place of rendezvous, which the Comte d'Artois willingly lent to his friends. One of them recalls in his memoirs a boudoir whose walls, floor and ceiling were entirely of mirrors. He notes with relish the embarrassment this caused to the ladies he took there, 'who had no other option but hastily to clasp their dresses into a semblance of trousers'. Such anecdotes give the inscription above the door – *Parva Sed Apta*, Small But Suitable – a wealth of possible connotations. If you peer through the windows of this charming building, you can still see plenty of mirrors along its walls, waiting vainly to reflect a way of life as remote from the twentieth century as the little château itself.

In the nineteenth century the Bagatelle passed for a time into the possession of Sir Richard Wallace, and the beautiful park in which it is set still has a distinctly English flavour. For an hour or so we can walk around the lawns, past streams and waterfalls and picturesque arrangements of shrub, ending up, perhaps, in front of the Orangerie, where a delightful flower garden stretches away towards the rotunda. From the security of this tranquil enclosure, it is somehow especially pleasant to be able to see the towers of La Défense rising in the distance.

At the edge of the Bois are two museums which could scarcely be more different in character. The MUSÉE NATIONALE DES ARTS ET TRADITIONS POPULAIRES, in the north, is a modern museum with an educational bias, designed according to the principles of the anthropologist Claude Lévi-Strauss. Part of it is given over to the severely academic *galeries d'étude* where students can come to make a detailed study of, as it might be, cow bells or peasant costumes. The other part of the museum, where the displays are grouped under the headings of Universe or Society, is intended for the general public. Even if you do not make much of the educational principle behind these arrangements, you can scarcely fail to be intrigued by some of the exhibits. One section, for example, follows the process that leads from earth to earthenware pottery, another takes us through the stages that lead from the corn to the baguette. (Croissants, it seems, owe their shape to the raising of the siege of Vienna by the Turks in 1693.) Elsewhere *son et lumière* effects bring to life a carpenter's house from 1852, laid out as it was in 1930, and a mountain cottage from the early years of the twentieth century. The museum is slightly awkward to reach but worth a visit. You are unlikely ever to have been in one quite like it.

By contrast, the MUSÉE MARMOTTAN, a handsome house not far from the Porte de la Muette, is very much an old-style museum, which is only just beginning to come to terms with modern expectations. Built up of a number of collections, of which the first was that of Jules Marmottan in the nineteenth century, it has both the attractions and the irritations of its mixed ancestry. While some of the ground-floor rooms are rather a jumble, with a number of the objects and paintings unlabelled, the floor above is both better lit and better laid out, thanks to the support of *The Reader's Digest*. Its enticing mixture of paintings ranges from sixteenth-century Dutch allegory to nineteenth-century views of Paris. Downstairs again, you can look at the collection of lovely medieval miniatures – French, Flemish and Italian – which make up the Wildenstein collection, before moving on to the museum's display of Monets, most of them housed in a room that has been excellently refurbished by Yosoji Kobayashi, Chairman of Nippon TV. The majority of these Monets are late paintings, often depicting views of the artist's garden at Giverny. The *Pont Japonais* of 1918 stands out among the several versions which are exhibited. One Monet that you will not be able to see is his *Impression – Soleil levant*, from which the Impressionists derived their name. Along with a number of other paintings, it was stolen from the museum in 1985.

From the Musée Marmottan we can wander through the Jardin du Ranelagh, inspired by its namesake in eighteenth-century London, and on to the Chausée de la Muette. We are now in the heart of the 16th arrondissement. There is nothing much in the quiet streets of Passy and Auteuil to draw attention to them. Their wealthy residents do everything possible to guard themselves against vulgar intrusion. An address in this area is the Parisian equivalent of

Gustave Caillebotte, The place de l'Europe. *Caillebotte was a talented amateur painter and an important collector of Impressionist paintings, particularly those of Monet.*

getting into the kingdom of heaven, and from the outside looks just about as boring. Most of the buildings, apart from the new blocks, were put up around the turn of the century, many in the 1890s. But they share none of the dubious glamour of that decade. The watchword here is respectability. Evil, when it is done, is done behind closed doors.

The only thing that has happened in the past few years to attract the tourist trade to this exclusive region is the publication of a little book by Thierry Mantoux called *BCBG*. From this came the tedious obsession with *Bon Chic, Bon Genre*, the game being to spot the preppy-looking youths and their opposite numbers with the glassy faces, the pearl necklaces and the foulards from Hermès. It already seems sadly dated.

In an odd way, the fact that so little goes on in these streets makes them particularly tiring to walk through, but since we are here we might look in on the spectacle museum a few yards down the avenue Mozart from Muette. For some reason there are an extraordinary number of opticians around here, and in one of them, Pierre Marly, you will find this curious little museum. It has no commercial designs on you; it is simply the tribute an enthusiast has paid to his craft. On display are examples of the eye-glasses affected by the *Incroyables* and the *Muscadins* at the end of the eighteenth century, some Venetian lorgnettes from the same period, a number of unlikely specimens from the Far East, some fine spectacles designed for short-sighted dogs, and a range of different sorts of eye-glass belonging to famous people from George Sand to Sophia Loren, and Sarah Bernhardt to Giscard d'Estaing. It is an unpretentious place; in all probability the elegant Parisian discussing the details of her new frames, whom you pass on your way out, will be quite unaware of the museum's existence.

We are heading back now towards the left bank, but there is one more museum to visit before we leave the seizième. Among the most attractive in this part of Paris, the little MUSÉE BALZAC is strategically placed between the rue Raynouard and the rue Berton. Strategically, because this was the house where Balzac lived from 1841 to 1847 at one of the many periods when he was under threat from the debt collector. Since he was also anxious to avoid service in the National Guard, the house's two exits on to different streets were a strong recommendation. In 1841 Balzac settled here under the name of M. de Brugnol, and over the next six years produced some of his greatest works, notably *Splendeurs et misères des courtisanes* and *La Cousine Bette*. The house itself is a pleasantly eccentric spot built on a slope. Inside you can see editions of his works and a variety of memorabilia, including his writing table and chair, the inkwell symbolically shaped like a padlock, which kept him at his desk, and the Limoges cafetière that sustained him through the long nights of writing. A hint of the dandy is suggested by his two canes, one of them set with turquoises, and the smart waistcoat which looks as though it has since been recut to fit someone several sizes smaller.

This part of the seizième is full of interesting little alleys, lanes and stairways, but it has been somewhat spoiled by the plethora of ugly apartment buildings put up earlier in the century. Almost opposite Balzac's house was the hôtel, on the corner of the rue Singer, where Benjamin Franklin carried out his experiments with a lightning conductor. Since the building was knocked down 80 years ago, only an act of exceptional piety will take people to the site today.

The rue Berton, along the bottom of Balzac's house, is a cobbled alley on the other side of which are the grounds of the Turkish Embassy, invisible but for the iron gates and the shady, tree-lined drive. Built at the end of the seventeenth century, this hôtel later became the home of the Princesse de Lamballe, whose loyalty to Marie-Antoinette led her to a particularly horrible death during the Revolution. For the last half of the nineteenth century the house was an asylum, run for most of that time by Dr Emile Blanche, who treated both Guy de Maupassant and Gérard de Nerval. Maupassant later died here in 1893. So close to the city's most famous monument, it can hardly have been an ideal site for someone who disliked the Eiffel Tower enough to eat at the restaurant there on the grounds that it was the only place in Paris from which one could be sure of not seeing the tower itself.

In front of the Turkish Embassy the rue d'Ankara slopes down towards the Seine, where it meets the avenue du Président-Kennedy, an unofficial race-track on which the Parisian male can advertise his tremendous potency. From the other side of the road, if you get across in one piece, you can see on the left bank of the river a clutch of skyscrapers and in mid-stream, at the tip of the island known as the allée des Cygnes, just visible between the metal struts of the charmless railway bridge, a scaled-down replica of the Statue of Liberty. Bartholdi's giant original was given to the United States by France in 1886. This miniature version, sited on the pont de Grenelle, was a return gift from America.

At this point, however, few visitors are likely to have much time for things American. A stone's throw away is the bizarre structure which in the mere hundred years of its life has come to symbolize Paris more decisively than any of her older, more venerable monuments. The EIFFEL TOWER looms even larger in the Paris of our imagination than it does in reality. To reach it we can simply stroll back towards the pont d'Iéna.

One's heart sinks at the prospect of saying anything at all about the Eiffel Tower. Not that I dislike it, but what is there to say about it? Does anyone really want to know that it is 1,052 feet high, that it weighs 9700 tonnes, that it is fastened by 2.5 million rivets, that it has 1652 steps, that it takes 50 tons of paint to cover it? I must have read statistics of this kind a hundred times without one of them registering for more than five minutes. Better to leave it all floating in the realm of the imagination. Though if this had been the general view, the tower would have been torn down long ago. Built by Gustave Eiffel for the Paris Exhibition of 1889, it originally had only a twenty-year lease on life. In the first year almost 2,000,000 people visited it, but by 1909 its popularity was on the wane. 'Few visitors,' noted E.V. Lucas in that year, 'ascend even to the first stage and hardly any to the top.' Fortunately, it was saved by its use for wireless telegraphy.

The ride to the top is a sardine experience in the tourist season. As an alternative, the poor, the impatient, the claustrophobic and the mean can take to the

'Going up in the lift I had a feeling in the pit of my stomach as if I were on a ship at sea,' wrote Edmond de Goncourt in his diary after a trip up the Eiffel Tower.

Seen from the Eiffel Tower, the Seine curves through the city.

stairs, at least to the second stage. The continuous spiral tends to be dizzying rather than exhausting, but there are in any case plenty of posters on the way up, detailing the history and construction of the tower, which give one a respectable excuse for stopping to catch one's breath. The first time, of course, everyone must go to the top, but on subsequent visits the second stage will probably be far enough. The view is what one is after, and once a certain height has been reached, the law of diminishing returns comes into operation. Indeed, hardened tourists may feel that by the time they have got as far as the restaurant on the first floor, they have done all that common sense requires. My only real reservation about the tower concerns its colour. Whatever claims are made for its technological importance, the true appeal for most people is quite obviously its total lack of function. Planted beside the Seine with no discernible purpose, this gigantic structure is an object that borders on the surreal, and surely it deserves something with a touch more fantasy than the various shades of brown and rust in which it has been solemnly reclothed every seven years since its birth.

One of the less energetic ways of paying homage to the Eiffel Tower is by admiring it from a bench in the Champ de Mars. This expanse of open ground behind the tower is a truncated version of what was intended as a parade ground for the students of the École Militaire at the far end of the Champ. Laid out in the eighteenth century, the Champ de Mars was initially capable of holding some 10,000 men. Although it was later enlarged to hold even more, it has tended to figure in the history of Paris for less military reasons – as the site of the first horse race, for example, and as the place from which the Montgolfier brothers made their first ascent by balloon. With the Revolution it became an ideal setting for the sort of public celebrations that one would normally make a longish detour to avoid, theatrical events such as the Festival of Federation and the Festival of the Supreme Being in which dignitaries of Church and State who were feeling uneasy about their necks joined hundreds of thousands of enthusiastic citizens in prolonged declarations of allegiance to the principles of the Revolution. In the nineteenth century the Champ reverted to the gentler spectacle provided by the occasional balloonist. Its present form dates from the 1920s, which saw the completion of the residential areas that had been built on part of its former terrain.

On our way towards the Invalides we might turn aside for a quick stroll past the stalls that line the cobbled southern end of the rue Cler. This is a place to note for future reference. As street markets go, it is, as one would expect in the 7th arrondissement, a reasonably decorous affair, in fact little more than an overflow from the shops. Nonetheless, you can find here some of the best fruit and vegetables in central Paris.

We turn now to what I have always found the most intimidating of the city's monuments. It is not just the huge scale of the INVALIDES that makes me hesitate, nor a rather limited enthusiasm for things military, it is above all a certain air of officialdom that seems to hang over the place, proclaiming itself, even before we reach the building, in the long stretches of bare lawn, fenced off from the public, which reach down to the river, unused and forbidding. But once one gets inside,

the majestic architecture exercises is spell. Built at the end of the seventeenth century to the design of Libéral Bruant, the Hôtel des Invalides was, and to some extent still is, a home for disabled soldiers, though it is now chiefly famous as the setting of the Musée de l'Armée and the site of Napoleon's tomb. We can approach it along the avenue du Maréchal-Gallieni, named for the military commander of Paris at the outbreak of World War I. When the Germans were advancing on Paris in 1914 and the French army was in disarray, Gallieni managed to save the city by commandeering over 1000 taxis and rushing them to the front with reinforcements for what became the first stages of the Battle of the Marne.

As you stand in the main courtyard, the *cour d'honneur*, look up at the dormer windows along the east side, on your left. The fifth one beyond the central pavilion has a curious image of a wolf's head poking through the decoration, while two paws clutch the top of the window. Here again we have one of the visual puns that embellish the buildings of Paris, a reference in this case to the man who supervised the construction of the Invalides, Louvois – *loup voit*/the wolf sees.

It is with good reason that the MUSÉE DE L'ARMÉE, which surrounds this courtyard, allows you to use its ticket on two consecutive days. The place is huge. Sabres, lances, guns, cannons, armour, flags, medals, badges, saddles, uniforms – if these are the kind of items that appeal to you, you will find them here in abundance, case after case of them, lavishly displayed. Many of the uniforms are

The façade of the Hôtel des Invalides, guarded by cannon and appropriately regimented bushes. Founded in 1671, at one time it accommodated up to 6000 disabled or pensioned-off soldiers.

tremendously pretty. Leaving aside the hussars, as an inevitable first choice, I would myself have opted for the chasseurs d'Afrique or the zouaves. It comes as something of a shock to notice amid the finery the shattered breastplate of a carabinier killed at Waterloo, a grim reminder of what the *ultima ratio regum* is all about. For those of less warlike disposition, the musem also displays, somewhat unexpectedly, the dog Napoleon kept on Elba – a big white dog, slightly moth-eaten now about the head, but unmistakably friendly. Of particular interest in the twentieth-century galleries is a fascinating model of a World War I trench network – barely recognizable, perhaps, to those who endured the squalid reality, but instructive to those of us who can only guess what it must have been like from grainy photographs and searing memoirs. The top floor of the museum is given over to an intriguing series of relief maps, modelled with scrupulous care to show us, for example, Perpignan as it was 300 years ago, Strasbourg in 1836, or Saint-Tropez in 1716, without port, quay or church, a mere huddle of houses round the edge of the sea.

Before we move on to Napoleon's tomb, we shall want to glance into the church of SAINT-LOUIS, partly for the building itself, which was the work of Bruant and Mansart, but partly also for the display of captured enemy colours that hang from above the galleries, two lines of faded banners eloquent of a world of smoke and gunshot remote from anything the casual tourist would care to know. The banners were once more numerous, but when the British and Russian troops marched into Paris in 1814, the governor of the Invalides burned 1417 of them to prevent their being taken.

Napoleon's tomb comes as an anticlimax. Its setting, under the magnificent dome of Hardouin-Mansart, is worthy of something better. Designed by

Napoleon's tomb by Visconti in the Église du Dôme. He was finally interred here in 1861, some 40 years after his death.

Visconti, this elaborate tomb received the ashes of Napoleon in April 1861, just over twenty years after they had originally been deposited in the Invalides. In front of an over-ornate altar by Visconti a large hole opens on to the tomb below, which stands in the centre like some inscrutable object of worship. The arrangement is similar to a nest of Russian dolls, with the emperor's body encased in six coffins, which are in turn surrounded by a sarcophagus of red porphyry. For readers who collect such details, the innermost coffin is of iron and the succeeding ones of mahogany, lead, lead again, ebony and oak.

The walkway round the tomb is surrounded by ugly marble reliefs inscribed with pompous messages glorifying the emperor. Our attention is drawn to his justice, benevolence, concern for the quality of life, support for the Christian Church, advancement of education, and general value to humanity. As one of the more reticent inscriptions puts it, summarizing his influence:

> The principles of disorder fade away, deeds grow humble, factions come together, wounds heal, creation seems once more to come forth from chaos.

Turning east from the Invalides, we move into the heart of what was for long the hallowed ground of the Parisian nobility. Names like rue de Grenelle, rue du Bac, rue de l'Université, rue de Lille are still redolent of the secluded grandeur that lies behind the high walls and imposing doors of the 7th arrondissement. Most of the hôtels (the town houses of the rich) have now been turned into embassies, government offices or expensive apartments, but one at least remains open to the public. At 77 rue de Varenne, the HÔTEL BIRON is only a stone's throw from the Invalides, and since it also houses the MUSÉE RODIN, it demands an extended visit.

The hôtel was built in the eighteenth century for a prosperous wig-maker who had set his sights on joining the aristocracy. Marshal Biron, a general during the Revolution, who gave it his name, was only briefly resident here before being dispatched to the guillotine in 1793. Later the hôtel was unfortunate enough to fall into the hands of a community of nuns, whose Mother Superior, a religious vandal who has since been canonized, tore out most of its gorgeous panelling on the grounds that it smacked of material vanity. Then in the early years of the twentieth century the nuns were duly dispersed and the building was used as an official home for artists. Rodin, Rilke and Isadora Duncan all stayed here, as did Jean Cocteau. It was Rodin's agreement that at his death, which came in 1917, his works should be bequeathed to the state in lieu of rent. The result is the museum we are about to enter.

It is a fine thing to be here at 10 o'clock when the big green gates swing open and you walk towards the hôtel, with the glittering dome of the Invalides rising on your right. Inside you can study the whole range of Rodin's work. There is an admirable collection of portraits which run from early pieces like the woman in the flowered hat to the *grandes dames* who were his models 40 years later. In the main hall, next to *The Kiss*, is the late *Figure de Femme à mi-corps* with body twisting to the right and hair falling forward. There is no better illustration of the amazing vigour that Rodin somehow retained into his seventies. Among the sculptures I return to most eagerly are the studies of Balzac he made in the 1890s – one in particular, nude, pot-bellied, defiant. The same spirit is apparent in the cast of Balzac that can be seen in the gardens. With his cloak flung around him, he stands there, wrapped against the world but ready to face it. The statue was commissioned by the Société des Gens de Lettres, but when a plaster cast of it was exhibited in 1898, the resulting controversy was too much for the timid literary folk; they took fright and refused to accept it. 'Superb,' said Oscar Wilde, who visited the Salon after his release from prison. 'The leonine head of a fallen angel ... People howl with rage over it.'

Among other sculptures on display are works such as *Pygmalion and Galatea*, *Ugolino and his Children*, *Le Penseur* and the dazzling *Femme accroupie* of 1882. In spite of the number of exhibits, the museum is not overwhelming. Nor, for that matter, is the hôtel itself; it gives the impression of a place to be lived in. The gardens at the back are indifferently kept, but a primitive café at one side makes them a pleasant spot to linger, surveying the works by Rodin that are disposed around the paths. On the way out we can see his study for the Gates of Hell, a work whose tortured bronze seems to reflect an inferno of the suffering rather than the sinful. He worked on it intermittently for much of his life. Finally, we must pause near the entrance beside the *Burghers of Calais*. In 1347, after the town had withstood siege for almost a year, Edward III agreed to spare it on condition that six burghers were handed over to him to do with as he chose. Through the intercession of Philippa of Hainaut they in the end escaped death, but Rodin depicts them as they are described by Froissart, men whose lives are to be forfeit, going to their execution with bare heads and bare feet, nooses about their necks, carrying the keys to the city and the castle. Of the six, one remains unbowed, legs straight, mouth set, eyes gazing ahead. This was the mayor of the city, Jean d'Aire.

In truth, the Faubourg Saint-Germain is not a particularly rewarding area for the footsore tourist. The streets are interminable, the buildings for the most part closed to the public, the gardens hidden, and the shops infrequent. It is perhaps moderately interesting to know that Talleyrand once lived in the Hôtel Matignon at number 57 rue de Varenne, now the official home of the French Prime Minister, that Mme du Deffand held her literary salon at 10–12 rue Saint-Dominique, now occupied by the Ministry of Defence, that Karl Marx lived at 38 rue Vaneau, that Alphonse Daudet died at 41 rue de l'Université, that Whistler painted at 110 rue du Bac and Saint-Simon wrote his memoirs at 102 rue de Grenelle, but in the end, unless one can get inside to see, the information does little to quicken the pulse.

Having said this, one must not be too hard on the Faubourg. It is, after all, a place of distinction, and it has one other charm so far unmentioned. Just before the rue de Grenelle meets the boulevard Raspail we come upon Bouchardon's Fontaine des Quatre Saisons. Voltaire objected that its site was too cramped, and one can see what he means. The only way to get a proper view of the fountain is to flatten oneself against the buildings on the other side of the street. In spite of this,

and the grossly flattering dedication to Louis XV, it is a charming piece of work. An elegant token of the eighteenth century, the Fontaine des Quatre Saisons marks a convenient boundary to the Faubourg Saint-Germain. Rarely can a city have been more sweetly personified than by the beautiful figure who here represents Paris, a world away from the heavy-bosomed Amazons who were to come into favour a century later.

4
The Left Bank and Montparnasse

....

THE MUSÉE D'ORSAY *to* THE QUAI DES GRANDS-AUGUSTINS

The Musée d'Orsay, which opened at the end of 1986, is one of the most intriguing of Paris's new museums. In Britain, where it is hard enough to get money to patch up the roof of the British Museum, such a project would have foundered on the drawing board; but France has a tradition of spectacular public ventures in the arts. This one was inspired. The old buildings of the Gare d'Orsay and the adjoining Orsay Palace Hotel seemed ripe for demolition. Like Baltard's pavilions in Les Halles, they had outlived their usefulness. Speculators talked enthusiastically of replacing them with a large new hotel. What in fact took place was a brilliant reworking of the original structure to provide a home for French art from 1848 to World War I. In other words, the collection neatly bridges the gap between the Louvre and the Pompidou Centre. The period itself is an absorbing one, and the old railway station, built for the Universal Exhibition of 1900, is both a product of that period and a wonderfully contrived setting for its works of art. In fact, the one drawback of the arrangement is that the fascinations of the building can sometimes seem a distraction from its contents.

The ground floor of the MUSÉE D'ORSAY is devoted to the period of the Second Empire, which, apart from more conventional art, produced paintings like Courbet's *Burial at Ornans* and Manet's *Déjeuner sur l'Herbe*. Manet tried to exhibit his painting at the Salon in 1863 but it was refused, becoming at least partly responsible for the creation of the *Salon des Refusés*. If you want to get an idea of the sort of stuff that was being accepted, walk across to the other side of the hallway and have a look at Cabanel's *Birth of Venus*, which was one of the great successes of that year. Its expanses of pastel flesh surrounded by tumbling cherubs are a fair sample of French *art officiel* in the mid nineteenth century. Elsewhere on the ground floor, along with work by Daumier, Delacroix, Ingres and Corot, you can see Whistler's much celebrated, and much reviled, portrait of his mother, entitled *Arrangement in Grey and Black no 1*. After an initial rejection by the Royal Academy, it was finally exhibited there, but to scant acclaim. ('The canvas

OPPOSITE *The graceful arches of the seventeenth-century pont Royal leading across to the Musée d'Orsay.*

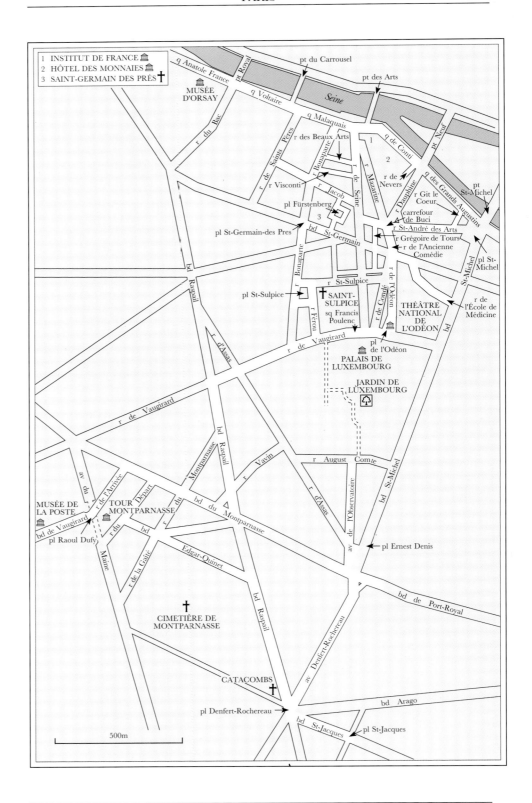

1 INSTITUT DE FRANCE
2 HÔTEL DES MONNAIES
3 SAINT-GERMAIN DES PRÉS

THE LEFT BANK AND
MONTPARNASSE

The former Gare d'Orsay seems an apt home for Claude Monet's Gare Saint-Lazare *of 1877.*

is large, and much of it vacant,' *The Times* noted perceptively in 1872. 'The picture has found few admirers among the thousands who seek to while away the hours at Burlington House, and for this result the painter has only to thank himself.') In the same area is Henri Fantin-Latour's *Un Coin de Table*, showing an unusually dignified Paul Verlaine at the left hand side, with next to him the young, full-lipped Arthur Rimbaud, his shock of hair contrasting with the domed head of the older poet.

Most of the Impressionist paintings are displayed on the top floor, and this is one aspect of the museum that has rightly provoked criticism. They were put up here to take advantage of the natural light, but there is simply not enough room for them. As a result, we find works by Gauguin, Van Gogh, Pissarro and Vlaminck shoved away in a low-ceilinged corridor. Another cramped little room houses the Degas pastels. Seurat's *The Circus* and a number of Lautrecs, among them the picture of a woman adjusting her garter, seem likewise to have been stuffed in wherever space could be found. A lack of seats aggravates the general unsatisfactoriness.

The main Impressionist rooms are better, although still far from ideal. Here you can see most of the paintings that were once housed in the Musée du Jeu de Paume – and also, alas, most of the people who once filled that small museum to bursting point. But after all, it is worth putting up with a little discomfort to get another look at pictures like Renoir's *Bal au Moulin de la Galette*, Degas' *L'absinthe*, Monet's *Le Déjeuner* and Van Gogh's *Portrait of Dr Gachet*.

Frédéric Bazille's Artist's Studio, rue de la Condamine *contains portraits of Zola, Renoir, Manet and Monet. Bazille himself, the tall figure next to the easel, was painted in later by Manet.*

The least crowded part of the Musée d'Orsay is usually the middle level, and it should not be missed. In addition to some fine early twentieth-century paintings – Rousseau's haunting *The Snake Charmer* hangs here – it has an excellent section on art nouveau, the style which left its mark on Paris in the curving plant motifs of the old Métro stations. The man responsible for them, Hector Guimard, is also represented here by some of the furniture he designed.

Unlike most museums, the Musée d'Orsay has a beautiful restaurant, which was once the dining room of the old Orsay Palace Hotel. For more modest budgets, the café on the top floor is also in its way an unusual spot. One wall has at its centre the reverse side of the station clock, so you can enjoy the curious experience of reading the time back-to-front while you drink your coffee. Afterwards, there is the bonus of a long balcony, opening off the café, which looks across the Seine towards northern Paris. For those who are more used to surveying the city from Montmartre, this offers a pleasurable change of direction.

From the Musée d'Orsay we can wander beside the Seine along the stylish quai Voltaire, lined with antique shops and galleries. Ingres, Delacroix and Corot all lived here and are all now represented in the neighbouring museum. (Ingres in fact died at 11 quai Voltaire on 14 January, 1867.) Among other residents, some of them commemorated by plaques, are Wagner, de Musset, Baudelaire, Sibelius, Montherlant, Oscar Wilde and, of course, Voltaire himself, who died in the house on the corner of the rue de Beaune, at number 27. My own favourite is a rather different sort of character, whose story is mentioned by the historian Jacques Hillairet. The Marquis de Bacqueville lived at the far end of the quay, just beyond the pont du Carrousel. He was one of Paris's early bird-men. Equipped with home-made wings, he attempted in 1742 to glide from the roof of his home at number 1 to the other side of the Seine. In the event he dropped on to a laundry boat and broke his thigh, but as such things go, it was a moderately successful venture. There is something oddly engaging about these quixotic figures who set out to defy gravity and transform themselves into birds. (The ill-fated optimist who tried to float down from the Eiffel Tower by means of pneumatic trousers was another of them.) It would be difficult to find a more vivid image of the hopeless aspirations that make us human. The marquis himself came to an appropriate end. When his house caught fire, he remained there to defend it against looters, a pistol in each hand, until the flames caught him and he died.

The imposing dome a short distance away, in front of the pont des Arts, belongs to the INSTITUT DE FRANCE, home of a number of academies of which the most famous is the Académie française. If the outside world tends to take members of the Academy, the 'Immortels', rather less seriously than they take themselves, that is perhaps no more than could be said of the members of most institutions. Their regular pursuits include the supervision of the official French dictionary, and they conduct their meetings with uncompromising ceremony. It is true, as everyone points out, that the list of those excluded from the Académie française constitutes a roll-call of the most celebrated names in French literature, more famous by far than most of those found worthy of inclusion. But on the other hand, the pomp and circumstance with which these very mortal *Immortels* surround themselves makes its own contribution to the respect which France accords the life of the intellect. Without it, for example, there might be more difficulty in sustaining a major radio network called *France Culture* – imagine the fate of a British or American equivalent.

Cardinal Mazarin provided the money for the Institut, which was built in the seventeenth century to the design of Louis Le Vau, the same architect who built many of the finest hôtels on the Île Saint-Louis. One casualty of the project was the Tour de Nesle, part of the Duc de Berry's hôtel, which had to be demolished to make way for the new building. The reputation of the medieval tower had long been stained by dark rumours about the orgies conducted there in the early fourteenth century by the three princesses of Burgundy, Marguerite, Jeanne and Blanche, who were said to have had their exhausted lovers thrown in sacks into the Seine. In another part of the Hôtel de Nesle, demolished at the same time, Benvenuto Cellini had his workshop in the middle of the sixteenth century.

Just beyond the Institut is the HÔTEL DES MONNAIES, an eighteenth-century building which houses the MINT. Fulsome tributes in the visitors' book suggest that its instructive museum is all that the devotee could require. Details of French currency from the ancient Gauls to the modern ten-franc piece are presented here according to a new system whereby coins are set in glass panels, so that both sides can be seen by the visitor. The untutored layman might be inclined to feel a sneaking preference for the flamboyant bank-notes from Indo-China.

It's worth strolling to the end of the quai de Conti to have a glance up the rue de Nevers. With its hefty walls and grudging windows, this oppressive relic of the Middle Ages is a striking antidote to romantic visions of medieval Paris.

Running south from the place de l'Institut is the attractive rue de Seine, packed with the small art galleries that have colonized the district. A short way up, it is linked to the rue Bonaparte by the Rue des Beaux-Arts and, parallel to it, the rue Visconti. The first is primarily a place of pilgrimage for those who wish to see the hotel at number 13, then called the Hôtel d'Alsace, in which Oscar Wilde died. It was a rather less salubrious place in the early years of the century than it is now, a world away from the hotel on the rue de Rivoli where Wilde had spent part of his honeymoon or the one on the quai Voltaire where he had stayed in the days of his triumph. Abandoned by all but a handful of friends, he returned to Paris in his closing years to lead a life of squalid isolation. His biographer, Richard Ellmann, conveys the characteristic tone of this period in the account of Wilde's meeting with a young American college student from Arkansas. Wilde had cadged a drink from him at a café in the rue Saint-Honoré, but within a few minutes a righteous onlooker came up to the youth and dropped a card saying, 'That is Oscar Wilde.' To prevent further embarrassment Wilde left. When the American wrote to his mother that he had actually spoken to this monster of depravity, he was ordered home by the next boat. It was in this sort of atmosphere that Wilde dragged out his final months, sustained partly by the kindness of the proprietor of the Hôtel d'Alsace, where he died on 30 November, 1900. 'I can't stand this wall-paper,' he is supposed to have said. 'One of us will have to go.'

The rue Visconti is a narrow, high-walled street, dotted with houses from the sixteenth and seventeenth centuries. In one of them, number 24, Racine spent the last seven years of his life. Another, number 16, was the home of the great actress Adrienne Lecouvreur. (Voltaire was beside her in this house when she died.) The building on the other side of the street, comprising numbers 17 and 19, is of more recent construction. It was here that Balzac set up his printing press in 1826, one of his many speculations that ended in debt. Like much of Paris, the rue Visconti has recently been dusted down and now shows cleaner walls and signs of increasing prosperity. Inevitably, its rising fortunes have been marked by the appearance, towards the rue de Seine, of the familiar art galleries.

Running past the opposite end of the street is the rue Bonaparte. It is a typical street of the 6th arrondissement, an agreeable mixture of shops selling fabrics, antique furniture, rare books and the like, interspersed with yet more art galleries. Like the rest of the area, it is saturated with memories of the intellectual life of Paris between the wars. The café, Le Pré aux Clercs, on the corner of the rue Jacob, was then a restaurant patronized by Hemingway, and a few doors further on, at number 36, is the Hôtel Saint-Germain-des-Prés, once the home of the philosopher Auguste Comte and later the place where Janet Flanner wrote her fortnightly 'Letter from Paris' for the *New Yorker*. Henry Miller and Jean Cocteau were at various times fellow guests.

Before we walk on to this southern end of the rue Bonaparte, we must cast an eye along the sober pavements of the rue Jacob, which crosses it just beyond the rue Visconti. This too was a street well known to the expatriate generation between the wars, particularly the Hôtel Jacob et d'Angleterre at number 44,

ABOVE *A house-front at the northern end of the rue de Nevers might give the lie to romantic illusions of medieval Paris.*

OPPOSITE *The Musée d'Orsay's balcony provides wonderful views across Paris towards Sacré-Coeur and Montmartre in the north.*

where Hemingway stayed when he first came to Paris. (It was in the Brasserie l'Escorailles, then called the Michaud, on the corner of the rue Jacob and the rue des Saints-Pères that Fitzgerald allegedly confided to Hemingway his doubts about the size of his penis. After a quick check in the Brasserie's lavatory, Hemingway said that he had nothing to worry about and urged him to make a comparative study of the statues in the Louvre. Later, confidences between writers being what they are, this became a diverting scene in the memoirs of Paris that Hemingway recorded in *A Moveable Feast*.) On the other side of the rue Bonaparte, number 20 rue Jacob was the home of Natalie Barney, where she held a literary salon known for its lesbian following, which, according to Samuel Putnam, was 'the one real salon in all Paris'. Its ground floor is now occupied by a charming shop that specializes, appropriately enough, in jewellery and other decorative items from the late 1920s. Among earlier visitors to Paris, Wagner, Benjamin Franklin and Laurence Sterne all stayed in the rue Jacob.

Towards the eastern end of the street, a short way beyond number 20, the narrow rue Fürstenberg leads off to the right and takes us into what is still one of the most delightful squares in Paris. Both street and square were built at the end of the seventeenth century by the Cardinal Fürstenberg who gave them his name. Sandwiched between the rue Jacob and the rue de l'Abbaye, the little *place*, with its paulownia trees and its five-globed lamp, has an atmosphere of delicious seclusion. All it lacks is a few benches. In summer, the trees create a canopy that keeps it perpetually in tranquil shade, as though the blinds have been drawn. Its most famous occupant was the painter Delacroix, who lived at number 6 from 1857 until his death in 1863. Today the house is a museum devoted to his work.

For some time now we have been circling the hub of this enchanting district without actually setting foot there. Like the boulevard Saint-Michel, the place Saint-Germain-des-Prés sums up in its very syllables a whole stratum of Paris life, both the period and the milieu. In the years after World War II this tiny area of central Paris was the focus of French, indeed of European, intellectual life. In the cafés and jazz cellars of Saint-Germain-des-Prés a post-war form of existentialism, developed by Sartre and Merleau-Ponty, was argued, explained and embraced by a whole generation of young Paris intellectuals.

Some of the familiar names still remain, though the clientèle is greatly changed. At the bottom of its overpriced menu the alluring Café des Deux Magots proclaims itself 'le Rendez-Vous de l'élite intellectuelle', but a glance round the tables, scattered with maps, phrase-books, cameras and picture postcards, suggests that, at least in summer, matters of the intellect are not high on the agenda for most of its customers. The Café de Flore, with its green and gold tables, maintains a slightly more austere aspect. It is altogether characteristic that a notice inside should request clients not to smoke scented tobaccos in their pipes, on the grounds that these might incommode some of the customers – who are presumably used to sterner stuff. Across the road the Brasserie Lipp is seen by many as a somewhat intimidating proposition, partly because of an overworked reputation for exclusivity. Regulars head indoors for their *choucroute garnie*, leaving the glassed-in terrace bare of all but a few resolute tourists. On a different footing, the jazz club Le Tabou, once frequented by Juliette Greco and Boris Vian, survives in the rue Dauphine, although it is now transformed into a discothèque. Perhaps more significant than these echoes of past glory is the general atmosphere of the district. It is richer and glossier than it used to be – redolent of the 1990s rather than the 1950s – but the area round Saint-Germain still pulses with a sense of life, of people who are young and unmortgaged and interested in talking for the sake of talking.

The prominence into which Saint-Germain-des-Prés was thrust after the war would have been unlikely to disconcert it. When most of Paris was wasteground or grazing land for cattle, Saint-Germain was already the site of a powerful Benedictine abbey, which became in time an important intellectual centre. The Revolution put an end to the abbey, but the church of SAINT-GERMAIN-DES-PRÉS survives, the oldest in Paris, with parts dating back to the eleventh century. Used as a dump for explosives in the Revolution, the church suffered less than most until a fire in 1794 left it vulnerable to the attentions of nineteenth-century restorers, whose work is evident in the polychrome decorations of the interior. The ambulatory, which has been stripped of its nineteenth-century paintwork, now gives the best impression of the church's earlier appearance. Note also the tombs of Descartes and Boileau in chapels off the ambulatory, and on the right of the entrance a fourteenth-century statue of Our Lady of Consolation. The marble columns in the triforium are a relic of the original church built by Childebert in the sixth century.

The term flying buttress has a peculiar charm. It is one of those happy instances where the concept, the expression and the object itself all seem absolutely right – daring, elegant and functional. And here at Saint-Germain-des-Prés, as at Notre-Dame, Paris can claim some of the earliest examples in Europe. To admire them in comfort we have only to take a seat outside the Café-Restaurant Apollinaire. (The poet's memory is incidentally rather better served by this café than by the ugly monument to him in the little garden just north of the church.)

Cutting across the site of the thirteenth-century abbey is the boulevard Saint-Germain. We shall be returning to it later, but for the moment you should leave the boulevard and head south towards Montparnasse. On the way, you might take a couple of minutes to have a look at an unlikely work of art presented to Paris by the province of Quebec in 1984. It has been placed on the south side of the boulevard in what is now the place du Québec. The broken bronze paving slabs achieve a sort of *trompe-l'oeil* effect which forces the passer-by to make a quick double-take before registering that this is in fact a novel form of fountain. It's a charming and ingenious idea, giving the fountain a spontaneous life which seems to have erupted from underground.

Nearby, the continuation of the rue Bonaparte will take us up to the place Saint-Sulpice. The square is pleasant enough, and yet there is something about the enormous church that makes the whole place difficult to love. Too much religion, perhaps. The curé of Saint-Sulpice who refused to accept Voltaire's corpse

The ambulatory of Saint-Germain des Prés contains both romanesque and gothic elements: the polychrome decoration of the arcade was added in the nineteenth century.

was part of a tradition of self-conscious piety that is still reflected in some shops around the square specializing in the sort of devout knick-knacks – Bernardette looking skywards with a tear, Joseph gazing unctuously down at the crib, little putti blowing trumpets – which breathe a decidedly cloying religiosity.

In front of the church the fountain known as the Quatre Points Cardinaux makes a mischievous pun at the expense of the prelates sculpted at its four cardinal points, none of whom achieved the rank of cardinal and who were therefore *point* (not at all) 'Cardinaux'. The classical façade of SAINT-SULPICE, with its curiously mismatched towers, makes an odd contrast to the highly decorated interior, which owes more to Jesuit tastes. It was in this elaborate setting that Camille Desmoulins, one of the early leaders of the Revolution, married Lucile Duplessis in 1790. Especially striking is the pair of holy water stoups formed from huge shells, similar to the ones presented by Victor Hugo to the church of Saint-Paul-Saint-Louis in the Marais (p. 142). These were a present from Venice to François I, and their attractive supports were carved in the eighteenth century by

Pigalle. In the first chapel on the south side are paintings by Delacroix. On the left wall Jacob is engaged in what looks like an aggressive waltz with the angel, while on the right a typically spiralling composition depicts Heliodorus driven from the temple. Details of the painting on the vaulting, which shows St Michael killing the dragon, are now all but invisible. With numerous interruptions Delacroix was at work on the chapel from 1850 to 1861. Not the least of his problems was the church authorities, who initially refused to let him work on Sundays. Since the music of the offices was a cherished source of inspiration to him, this led to a prolonged, and eventually successful, campaign to get their pious decision reversed. In the end, the paintings were given only a tepid welcome. A notable exception to the general lack of enthusiasm was Baudelaire; but he, regrettably, praised them for exactly what the modern visitor is least able to see, the brilliance of their colours.

If you are in luck, you may find yourself in the church at a time when its vast organ is being played. With 6588 pipes it is among the biggest in the world. It fills the church with a richness of sound that can do much to reconcile the listener to a place that might otherwise seem excessive.

A short way beyond the place Saint-Sulpice, we make our first contact with the rue de Vaugirard. It is unlikely to be our last. The street is uninteresting but long, the longest in Paris. We can join it for a weary fraction of its length as we head southwards. This is one part of the walk where there is little chance of getting lost, for our goal looms above almost every other structure in the city. The TOUR MONTPARNASSE is 688 feet high, not to mention another 230 feet sunk in the earth to provide the foundations. It would be hard to think of another building in Paris, including the Pompidou Centre (pp. 136–8), which has been more execrated. Rather unjustly, it seems to me. As skyscrapers go, it is a good-looking one, elegantly shaped and interestingly tinted with bronze-coloured glass. But that begs the question of whether this is really the place for skyscrapers at all, and there I suppose the answer is no. It belongs in La Défense (p. 67). Somehow its overpowering presence has sucked the character out of much of the surrounding area. Around the base of the tower the new development has made of this part of Montparnasse an urban wasteland which is depressing to walk through. One should perhaps fall back on a variant of Maupassant's response to the Eiffel Tower: the best way to get clear of the ugly commercial centre in front of the Tour Montparnasse is to go up to the top and look out. From its fifty-ninth floor there is a panorama of Paris which, particularly at night, can transform the whole experience from the dispiriting to the exhilarating.

The imagination has to work fairly hard in Montparnasse to recover much of the excitement of the early decades of the century when this was the main centre of artistic and bohemian life in the city. Its association with the arts dates back to the early 1600s when Queen Margot took over the district just to the north of Saint-Germain, which had formerly belonged to the university and been called the Pré-aux-Clercs. Driven out of their stamping-ground beside the river, the students retreated to this area in the south, where debris from the ancient quarries had thrown up a hillock that was by then covered with grass. Since it provided a setting where poetry could be declaimed and matters of the intellect discussed without interference, it was dubbed ironically the Mount of Parnassus.

Three centuries later, when the focus of artistic life in the city began to shift from Montmartre to the Left Bank, Montparnasse again came into its own. Names like the Dôme, the Coupole, the Rotonde, the Sélect can still stir images of Modigliani hawking canvasses from table to table among a sceptical clientèle, of Apollinaire holding forth to a mixed crowd of painters and poets, of young Americans drunk on wine and literature and freedom from America, of Man Ray and Kiki de Montparnasse watching the sky lighten over Paris at the end of the night, of Simone de Beauvoir recording the slow progress of war from one of the café tables. But the images, and the cafés, are a long way from the Montparnasse of the 1990s. The Dôme and the Rotonde still eye each other across the boulevard du Montparnasse, as do the Coupole and the Sélect, all within a stone's throw of the boulevard Raspail; and that is where the resemblance to the world of the 1920s and 1930s ends. Admirable food is still to be had at the Coupole, but its recent renovation has left the covered *terrasse* looking more like the site of a pizza parlour than a great café; the Sélect has grown more select – and more expensive; the Dôme and the Rotonde have likewise moved upmarket, edging towards the more dignified status of restaurants.

Since 1939 Rodin's statue of Balzac has presided over the dismal changes in the area, looking out from the cross-roads beside the Rotonde with eyes that are painful black holes.

For those who would welcome an imaginative stimulant after confronting the modern boulevard, this might be the moment for a detour to the rue de Dantzig in the south-west of Montparnasse. Number 2 passage de Dantzig was originally built as the Wine Pavilion for the 1900 Exhibition. Like an earlier, more famous exhibit, it was designed by Gustave Eiffel, and was later reconstructed to provide artists' studios in Montparnasse. Set back behind high iron gates which are softened by the ivy that trails over the top of them, it is an eccentric three-storey brick building whose distinctive shape at once explains its nickname of La Ruche, the Beehive. It was here that Modigliani, Chagall, Brancusi, Léger and others had their base.

Elsewhere in Montparnasse you might do worse than spend an hour in the modern MUSÉE DE LA POSTE, a short way from the tower, on the boulevard de Vaugirard. Entered from the fifth floor of the Maison de la Poste, it is so constructed that without quite realizing what is happening you gradually work your way downwards as you move from room to room, until you emerge at the end of the museum to find yourself almost back on the ground floor again. It is a surprisingly big museum, inventively laid out, with material that touches every kind of mail transport from horse to hot air balloon. Among items that might catch your eye are a formidable pair of postilion's boots which look quite large enough to disappear into, some resplendent uniforms of mid nineteenth-century postmasters, attractive models of various mail coaches, and a bewildering array of

OPPOSITE *The somewhat mismatched towers of Saint-Sulpice seen from the Tour Montparnasse.*

post-boxes from around the world. As you enter each room the lights spring on at your arrival, an arrangement which confirms one's suspicion that the place is not usually overcrowded. If you like slightly off-beat museums, then this is a good one to try. Don't miss the room devoted to the development of airmail, a wonderfully nostalgic mixture of Saint-Exupéry and *Casablanca*.

From here we can return past the Tour Montparnasse and continue on to the boulevard Edgar Quinet. Running east towards the Cimetière de Montparnasse this is one street that has largely escaped the skyscraper's baneful influence. It has an agreeably shabby, slightly provincial atmosphere that carries a welcome suggestion of earlier times. One landmark that has not survived is number 31, now a new and ugly apartment building above a new and ugly bank. To call it a landmark is perhaps misleading, though it was no doubt a landmark to some. Certainly it enjoyed a degree of notoriety in the late 1920s as the site of Paris's newest and most spectacular brothel. Le Sphinx, gleaming with fashionable chromium plate, was launched by a lavish party to which all potential customers in the neighbourhood were invited – along with their wives.

Further along the street, opening off to the right, is the rue de la Gaîté, seedy now as of old. At number 26, between a café and a new purple-and-black-fronted sex shop, you will find the somewhat dilapidated entrance to the old Théatre de la Gaîté-Montparnasse, where Colette performed her *poses plastiques*. On the other side of the boulevard Edgar Quinet, more literary ghosts haunt 7, rue Delambre, site of the Dingo bar (which later became the Auberge du Centre), where Hemingway and Scott Fitzgerald first met in 1925.

Curiously central to this whole district, both geographically and in terms of the hold it seems to have on the affections of the inhabitants, is the CIMETIÈRE DE MONTPARNASSE. Cemeteries are a form of tourist attraction which has never greatly excited me, but Paris is undoubtedly well supplied with them. This one at Montparnasse numbers among its dead Baudelaire and Sainte-Beuve, Maupassant, Franck, Tzara, Zadkine, Soutine, Sartre and, more recently, Simone de Beauvoir. Here, if you wish, you may wander among their graves.

A related entertainment, perhaps less specialized in its appeal, is on offer in the neighbouring place Denfert-Rochereau. Constructed out of the old tunnels and quarries left by the Romans, the CATACOMBS came into being towards the end of the eighteenth century, when the Cimetière des Innocents was closed and a dumping-ground was needed for the bones. After descending a spiral staircase which takes you to a depth of 20 metres below the street, you begin the visit with a long, slightly tedious walk through the tunnels. Just as it starts to seem like the sort of excursion to warn your friends against, a notice indicates that you have reached the ossuary. Over the entrance are written the words: '*Arrête, c'est ici l'empire de la Mort*'. A few more steps and you will see what it means. Suddenly you are walking through a maze of human bones. Tightly packed, they have a form which in the dim light is reminiscent of a flint wall. Some of the skulls are old now and crumbling, others are of more recent date. These bones are what is left of some five or six million Parisians who lived their individual lives, were buried in

Paris cemeteries and finally transferred here between 1785 and 1860. It is hard in this strange place to clothe the skulls with flesh and think that they were people. Hard too, as one walks past, with moisture dripping from the ceiling, to avoid such Hamlet-like reflections. Not the least startling aspect of the visit is a notice that warns you, as you emerge into the upper air again, that any bags you have with you may be searched to prevent theft.

At the margin of the city, this was for long a disreputable and somewhat dangerous area. When the gallows were moved from the place de Grève in 1832, it was the place Saint-Jacques, just to the east of Denfert-Rochereau, that became the place of public execution. Anyone who has seen Marcel Carné's film, *Les Enfants du Paradis*, will remember Marcel Herrand's portrayal of the dandified criminal, Lacenaire. This extraordinary figure, part anarchist, part crook, went to the scaffold here in 1836. Handsome, impeccably dressed, with a flower in his buttonhole, he refused the attentions of the priest and requested that his confederate be guillotined first, so that he could enjoy the details of the procedure. When his turn came, he managed somehow to twist round on the guillotine to allow himself the ultimate sensation of watching the blade descend on his own neck. The same blade he glimpsed at the moment of his death is now exhibited on a wall in the Conciergerie (p. 33).

There is little to draw us further south, unless we wish to visit Lenin's house at 4, rue Marie-Rose. This was where he lived from 1909 to 1912, and his apartment can be seen by appointment. Not far away from it is the PARC DE MONTSOURIS, its pretty rock gardens and well-kept lawns sloping down to an attractive lake patrolled by ducks. When the park was opened in 1878, this lake caused an unfortunate scandal by somehow draining itself of water on the very day of the inauguration. In his chagrin, the engineer who had been responsible for it committed suicide. Perhaps because of the neighbouring Cité Universitaire, the park is supervised with unusual vigilance by uniformed officials who are quick to blow their whistles at anyone reckless enough to try sitting on the lawns.

A cheering sight as we begin to walk back towards the Seine is the fountain by Davioud that dominates the place de l'Observatoire, its water, in Hemingway's words, 'rippling on the bronze of the horses' manes'. Apart from the horses, there is also a fine ring of turtles, front flippers in the air, shooting water vigorously back towards the centre of the fountain. The display must have been quite familiar to Hemingway, since the fountain stands in a small garden only a few yards from the Closerie des Lilas, where he wrote parts of *The Sun Also Rises*. Even nearer to hand, just outside the Closerie, is the statue of Marshal Ney, who was executed in 1815 for supporting Napoleon after his escape from Elba. The execution took place a short distance from where the statue stands, in front of the present number 43 on the other side of the avenue de l'Observatoire.

Like many of the cafés frequented by writers of the 1920s and 1930s, the Closerie des Lilas has moved relentlessly up-market, putting itself outside the range of most casual passers-by. Fortunately, the JARDIN DU LUXEMBOURG is near enough to provide the weary tourist with an ideal alternative. Even in the

A street of the dead in the Cimetière de Montparnasse.

*Davioud's Fontaine de l'Observatoire
was placed at the carrefour in 1875.*

height of summer it retains a refreshing atmosphere of tranquillity. It could scarcely be easier to recover the feeling that George Moore describes in his memoirs, looking back to the garden of the 1870s:

> I threw myself on a bench and began to wonder if there was anything better in the world worth doing than to sit in an alley of clipped limes smoking, thinking of Paris and of myself.

If we do the same today, we shall no doubt see around us the habitual denizens of the park – solitary figures feeding the pigeons, toddlers trying out their first steps, students working, elderly couples sitting in conversation, lovers, here as everywhere in Paris, twined in a permanent embrace. At the apex of the dusty paths is the wide octagonal pond with a single high jet of water from its centrepiece, around which float the model boats – many of them still powered by sail and hooked in with a stick – that give the place an agreeably anachronistic feel. Elsewhere in the garden, which has changed much since it was laid out in the seventeenth century, we can take one of the familiar green metal chairs and sit beside the Medici fountain to study the fate of Acis and Galatea represented there, or pause near the Orangerie in front of Dalou's monument to Delacroix, a whirl of dramatic activity that would surely have appealed to the painter.

Salomon de Brosse built the PALAIS DU LUXEMBOURG for Marie de' Medici, starting work on it in 1615. Her idea was to have a palace that would be built along the same lines as the Pitti in Florence. This is not quite how it turned out, but Marie herself was pleased with the result. After commissioning Rubens to paint some pictures for it, she took up residence in 1625. But enemies of Cardinal Richelieu could rarely look forward to a peaceful old age. Five years later, on 10 November, 1630, Marie forced her son Louis XIII to choose between herself and the cardinal. Convinced that she had at last gained the upper hand, she turned out merely to have overreached herself. This was the so-called Day of Dupes, and it left Richelieu firmly in control. Before long Marie was unceremoniously bundled off to Cologne, where she died in exile, forsaken and unmourned. Thereafter the palace enjoyed varied fortunes, becoming at different times a prison, a law court, a centre for the German Occupation and now the seat of the Senate.

If we leave the garden beside the palace, we shall find ourselves facing the back of what looks like a classical temple. It is in fact the THÉÂTRE NATIONAL DE L'ODÉON. The original theatre, which had put on Beaumarchais's *Marriage of Figaro* in 1784, was destroyed by fire at the end of the eighteenth century and rebuilt in 1808. After World War II it took to specializing in twentieth-century drama, and until the dismissal of its director, Jean-Louis Barrault, in 1968, it was hugely successful.

Sloping away from the theatre towards the boulevard Saint-Germain is the rue de l'Odéon. Notice on the right the wrought-iron sign beside the door of number 7. It was designed from a photograph of James Joyce and Adrienne Monnier, the woman who owned the bookshop that used to occupy these premises. 'La Maison des Amis du Livre', which Monnier started in 1915, provided an important literary meeting place between the wars, where writers like Valéry, Gide and Claudel came together to read and discuss their works. The sign has now been appropriated by the present owners of the site, the Galerie Saint-Germain-des-Prés. It was on the other side of the road, at number 12, that Monnier's friend Sylvia Beach installed her English language bookshop 'Shakespeare and Company'. Over the years it became famous for its support of expatriate writers, among them Pound, Hemingway and, above all, James Joyce, whose novel *Ulysses* was first published here in 1922.

The carrefour de l'Odéon is looked down on by the swaggering figure of Danton, who was arrested here, where his house once stood, in 1794. Today his statue marks one of the busiest spots on a busy street. The boulevard Saint-Germain has seen its fortunes rise as those of the *grands boulevards* on the right bank declined. Its line of cafés near the church of Saint-Germain-des-Prés offers as pleasant a spot for a drink on the *terrasse* as anywhere in Paris. On a summer evening the stretch of pavement beside the church is punctuated by musicians, painters, mime artists and conjurors, all doing their bit to keep the tourists happy, and hoping the tourists will reciprocate. It was near here that one of the early

anarchist outrages of the 1890s took place, when Ravachol, later to be guillotined, planted a bomb in number 136, the site of which is now occupied by a couple of fashionable clothes shops.

The streets which radiate from the boulevard Saint-Germain in this crowded little quarter are almost without exception worth exploring. Running off towards Saint-Michel is the rue de l'École-de-Médecine, where number 15, once the site of a Franciscan monastery, became the centre of the Club des Cordeliers, whose members included Danton, Marat and Desmoulins. Like most of the street, it has now been taken over by the University of Paris VI's faculty of medicine. It was in this same street that Marat was living when Charlotte Corday, who had travelled from Caen for the purpose, struck him down in his bath on 13 July, 1793.

On the other side of the boulevard, the rue de l'Ancienne-Comédie will take us down to the carrefour de Buci. This fascinating street derives its name from the old theatre of the Comédie-Française, which in 1689 had found a real tennis court at number 14 and established itself there for the next 80 years. Among those who benefited from the theatre was a young Sicilian, Francesco Procopio dei Coltelli, who had set up a café just opposite the tennis court a few years earlier. François Procope, as he chose to call himself when he got to Paris, had worked initially for a couple of Armenians who sold coffee as a novelty at the Saint-Germain fair. However far-sighted he was about its possibilities, he could hardly have envisaged that the café he opened in this street would still be in the same place, serving the same beverage, three centuries later. In the intervening years it has seen much. Patronized by Voltaire, Rousseau, Diderot and d'Alembert, it played its part in the birth of the *Encyclopédie*; during the Revolution it was a haunt of the members of the Club des Cordeliers; in the nineteenth century its customers included some of the greatest names in French literature, such as Musset, Sand, Balzac, Gautier, Verlaine and Huysmans. Today it is more of a restaurant than a café, but it offers a choice of menus that are reasonably enough priced to tempt anyone with a taste for its history.

The area round the carrefour de Buci is one of the most animated parts of the left bank, and has been since the days of Henri IV. Its streets pulsate with life from early in the morning until well after most people will want to be in bed (a point to be borne in mind when selecting one's hotel room in this district). Sprinkled with cafés and lined with stalls selling fruit and flowers, the stretch of the rue de Buci leading up to the rue de Seine becomes in summer an unofficial pedestrian precinct. If you wander along here in the evening, it is easy enough to come by a cheap meal. Try the rue Grégoire-de-Tours, for example, which has a representative selection of restaurants as well as an interesting old street sign at number 6, depicting a naked savage.

The history of the area is not without its darker side. Just to the east of the carrefour the cour du Commerce-Saint-André leads off to the right. At a workshop in this little passageway, running up behind the Procope, the guillotine was first developed and tested. Displaying all the tactlessness of an enthusiast, its inventor Dr Guillotin assured the National Assembly: 'With my machine I will have your

OPPOSITE *The wide expanses of the Jardin du Luxembourg make this garden a favourite with residents and visitors alike.*

heads off in the blink of an eye, and you will feel nothing more than a very slight coolness about the neck.' No doubt many members of the Assembly were later in a position to vouch for the accuracy of this. When it did finally make a public appearance in April 1792 in the place de Grève, the guillotine caused widespread dismay among a public that was used to more elaborate and luxurious spectacles. But the new machine soon made up in quantity what it lacked in quality – to such an extent that only the death of Robespierre prevented Guillotin himself from putting it to the test.

As we walk along the rue Saint-André-des-Arts, we shall pass at number 64, on the corner of the rue Mazet, the site of the old Porte Saint-Germain, later known as the Porte de Buci. In 1418 the Armagnacs were in possession of Paris and the Burgundians at its gates. On the night of the 28–29 May the son of the keeper of the Porte de Buci stole into his room while he slept, took the keys and opened the gate to the waiting Burgundians. What followed was a massacre of the Armagnacs that ranks among the bloodiest episodes in French history. Distinguished for their acts of slaughter were the members of the butchers' guild, a powerful group who supported the Duke of Burgundy. The Comte d'Armagnac was himself killed and a strip of his skin paraded around Paris in ghastly parody of the white scarf worn by his party.

A short way further down, you might notice the old stone street sign above the door of number 52; it is one of those from which the letters 'St' were erased during the Revolution. A few doors away, at number 44, is a chemist's shop that also deserves a mention. This particular building is only about a hundred years old, but there has been pharmacy on the spot for just over 300 years. It is not perhaps a matter of great importance, but if one is going to buy aspirin anyway, one might as well do it with a sense of history. Romantics, at least, will be gratified to think that people were stepping across the threshold for much the same purpose a hundred years before the Revolution.

To conclude the walk, we can continue to the end of the street and there pause for refreshment in the place Saint-André-des-Arts, whose cafés command an excellent view of the colourful life of the district. Alternatively, we might cut down one of the side-streets to the quai des Grands-Augustins, and then, if we are in funds – quite substantial funds – we could end the day at the beautiful Restaurant Lapérouse, on the corner of the oldest quay in Paris, looking out across the glittering Seine.

OPPOSITE *The Jardin du Luxembourg is dotted with neoclassical statuary. Devastated in the Revolution, the garden bears little resemblance to that laid out for Marie de' Medici.*

5
The Latin Quarter

....

BOULEVARD SAINT-MICHEL *to* SAINT-JULIEN-LE-PAUVRE

No one has much to say for the boulevard Saint-Michel these days. It was once the symbol of all that was daring and disreputable and alarmingly continental about Paris. To have lived on the boulevard Saint-Michel, even to have *stayed* on it, carried a wealth of exciting suggestion. It was a place of late nights, long hair and lost virginity – everything that mothers wanted to protect their children from. In James Joyce's *Ulysses* Stephen Dedalus practises dropping it casually into the conversation, 'When I was in Paris, boul' Mich' . . .' Back in the nineteenth century good provincial bourgeois would shake their heads knowingly on hearing of a neighbour's son who had taken lodgings in the Latin Quarter. The presence of the Sorbonne had turned this into the student district of Paris, and wherever students come together loose women and immoral talk are sure to follow. Since the time of François Villon in the Middle Ages, when students had been obliged to speak Latin (hence the name of the area), its reputation has always been slightly suspect.

Recently, the boulevard Saint-Michel has gone into a decline. Tourists still flock to it, but the writers of guide-books deplore the evil empire of McDonald and Burger King. In truth, the fast food places seem to have conquered the area with more than usual brutality, choosing along the way some particularly bilious colours for their plastic interiors. It is frequently assumed that these places are kept in business by philistine Americans, unable to survive for 24 hours without a burger and fries, but this is no more than partly true. While many young Americans will go to endless trouble to select authentic cafés and sit outside on the *terrasse* in all weathers, wishing themselves back to the Paris of Hemingway and Henry Miller, it is often their French counterparts who are queueing up to enjoy the doubtful pleasures of the fast food chains.

In spite of all this, I would still feel cheated if I had spent a weekend in Paris without at some time wandering over here. It is always lively, there is always something going on. In winter the smell of roasted chestnuts greets you as you

OPPOSITE *Saint-Étienne-du-Mont's sixteenth-century rood screen is the only one surviving in Paris.*

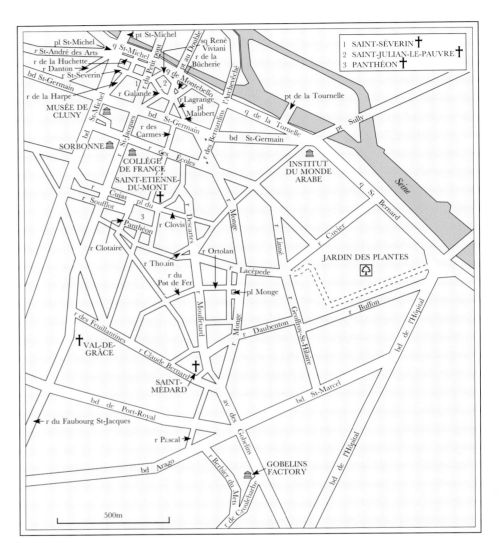

THE LATIN QUARTER

emerge from the Métro, mingling with the smells from the Greek and North African restaurants that line the neighbouring streets. If you turn up here at 6 in the evening there will be the usual milling assembly of shoppers and sightseers, with probably a crowd gathered at the corner of the rue de la Harpe round a fire-eater or a musician. If you turn up at 4 in the morning, there will still be little knots of people talking at the corners, couples strolling past who seem in no hurry to get home, a café or two where you can sit and watch the end of the night.

The apex of the boulevard's crowded life is the place Saint-Michel, where on a summer evening, among the young, the hip, the drunk and the stoned, with guitar music in the air, it can seem that time has stood still since the 1960s. The square is dominated by Davioud's statue of St Michael. This is not an inspiring piece, but it hardly deserves the contempt with which it is treated both by writers and by members of the public. Put up in 1860, it is a true product of its time. In the Second Empire furniture in the Musée des Arts Décoratifs you will find the same self-conscious dignity that has just tipped over into pomposity. It is a style in which everything aspires to the condition of a public monument; and the works that really are public monuments, like Davioud's statue, are all too aware of the fact. If you can clear a space among the *clochards* and back-packers, you might notice two plaques beside the water-spouting chimeras on either side of the statue. These commemorate the local Resistance fighters who were killed in the last days of the German Occupation between 19 and 25 August 1944. Clogged with empty lager cans, polystyrene cartons and abandoned bottles, the fountain does little to honour their memory.

We can wander up the boulevard and lament its decline some other day. This afternoon we shall turn back towards the river and stroll to the right along the quai Saint-Michel, enjoying the view of Notre-Dame. It needs to be an afternoon, because we are planning to pause at the *bouquinistes*. The weather-beaten green boxes which line the quays of the Seine in this area, especially along the left bank, are of mainly nostalgic interest today. Books have increasingly given way to tourist tat. Inside most of the chests you are likely to find a variety of commonplace paperbacks and uninteresting prints, mixed with model snow-storms and miniature Eiffel Towers. In earlier times, when exotic pornography was less easy to come by, they held a more vital interest for both Parisians and visitors. And for the collector of antiquarian books there was always the chance of a rare first edition that had gone unnoticed by the bearded old man who sat nearby in his folding chair waiting placidly for custom. This curious mode of selling books originated in the seventeenth century on the pont Neuf, when enterprising salesmen took advantage of the new pavements to set up temporary booths. Established booksellers objected strenuously, but the *bouquinistes* flourished and soon spread to the neighbouring quays, where they have kept a foothold ever since.

Just before you reach the Petit Pont, a narrow street opens to the right beside a bookshop of a more conventional kind. This dark little alley, which dates back to the sixteenth century, has one of the central gutters that are characteristic of the older parts of the city. Before the Revolution these channels down the middle of the street provided the standard means of disposing of waste. Everything from left-over food to the contents of chamber pots was chucked out of doors and windows into this gutter, where it would wait to get washed away. In the meantime it could provide a convenient trough for local pigs. The stench and filth can barely be imagined. Walking down here a couple of centuries ago, one would have kept well to the side.

Today the street is notable chiefly for its name, the rue du Chat-qui-Pêche. Until Napoleon promoted the system of numbering houses, most were identified, much as public houses still are in England, by signs above the door. Every street presented the passer-by with a battery of these signs, swinging from iron struts, carved over the door, painted on the wall, or displayed wherever there was room. Most of them have long since vanished, including the fishing cat from which this

Until the early nineteenth century many houses in Paris were identified by signs like this one in the rue Saint-Séverin.

street took its name, but elsewhere in the neighbourhood a number of the signs are still visible. At 13, rue Saint-Séverin, for example, you can see between the first-floor windows the carved image of a swan twining its neck around a cross. The building was actually called *Au Signe de la Croix*, At the Sign of the Cross, but the designer has played on the French word for swan, *cygne*, to produce this gentle visual pun.

Remains of a couple of similar signs can be seen in the attractive little rue de la Huchette, which we come to at the end of the rue du Chat-Qui-Pêche. It is hard now to visualize the rue de la Huchette as one of the most fashionable streets of the left bank, favoured in the sixteenth century by foreign ambassadors to the city, but it does nevertheless retain a flavour of its past history, and many of the buildings, such as the hôtel at number 10 where Napoleon took lodgings in 1795, are still intact. At the end of the 1920s it again became famous when the American journalist Elliot Paul wrote *A Narrow Street*, describing in affectionate detail the daily comings and goings of its mixed population of shopkeepers, prostitutes, artisans and eccentrics.

The area has been greatly changed over the past few years by pedestrian walk-ways, underground car parks and the general process of catering for tourists. Cheap restaurants seem to breed here like flies on a rubbish tip. Every time one turns round there are a couple more, all colourful, all noisy, all serving much the same food, all, or almost all, to be avoided by anyone wanting a decent meal. And yet, though I would not choose to eat here, I still find the atmosphere vaguely intoxicating – as, for different reasons, I used to do twenty years ago, when I looked out from one of the balconies of the old Hôtel de l'Europe on my periodic weekends of escape from England.

This is primarily a district for random wandering, but make sure that at some stage you reach the late gothic church of SAINT-SÉVERIN. The north entrance, facing the rue Saint-Séverin, is through a door in the thirteenth-century tower. Although the relief on the tympanum, which shows St Martin dividing his cloak with the beggar, belongs to the nineteenth century, the saint's association with the church goes back much further. In earlier times it was a custom amongst travellers to hang their horse-shoes on this façade as an ex-voto offering to him when they returned from a journey.

The interior of the church is not especially rich, but it has one feature that should not be missed: its remarkable double ambulatory. To understand what makes this so unusual, you must walk round until you draw level with the main altar, where twisting ribs of stone reach up from the pillars towards the vault, creating an effect that the French writer Huysmans compared to a forest of palm trees. And you can see exactly what he means – the impression of walking through a petrified arbour of palms is bewitching.

As you come out of the church, have a look at the main west entrance. Although it dates from the late thirteenth century, it was not actually built for Saint-Séverin. It belonged originally to the church of Saint-Pierre-aux-Boeufs on the Île de la Cité. When this church was demolished in 1839, the doorway was

OPPOSITE *The narrow rue de la Huchette preserves something of the character of earlier times.*

ABOVE *Part of the former gothic cloister of Saint-Séverin, later used as a charnel house.*

OPPOSITE *The courtyard of the Hôtel de Cluny, originally the official residence of the abbots of Cluny, and now a museum of medieval art.*

transported stone by stone and re-erected here at Saint-Séverin. If you study the wooden doors, you can still see interwoven among the foliage on the central panel the initials of the old church, SP.

Before leaving Saint-Séverin, you might glance through the iron railings at what used to be the cemetery on the south side of the church. At the far side are the remains of the cloister built at the end of the fifteenth century. This later became a charnel house, where the bodies were stacked in tiers between the arches. Nonetheless, people seemed quite happy to go on living in the apartments which had been built on top of it and which remained there until the eighteenth century. This cloister was the unlikely scene, in 1474, of Paris's first operation for the stone. The surgical procedures were still a matter of doubt, so it was tried out on a convicted criminal. Since he had anyway been condemned to death, it was felt that how he died was not of much consequence. As it turned out, the operation was a success and the patient was sent on his way a free man, cured of the stone and with money in his pocket.

Long before this became the student quarter of Paris, it was the centre of the old Roman town of Lutetia, and we can see some of the remains on the corner of the boulevard Saint-Michel and the boulevard Saint-Germain. For a more thorough inspection, we must turn to the neighbouring MUSÉE DE CLUNY. This fifteenth-century hôtel, the former residence of the abbots of Cluny, offers one of the highlights of a visit to Paris. Built on the site of the Roman baths, it now houses a superb collection of medieval art. Objects displayed range from locks and door-knockers to Viking swords and gold altarpieces. The hôtel itself is a perfect setting for its contents, complete with rounded turrets, armorial decorations and ancient well-head. The only cavil a visitor is likely to make is about the system of labelling, which depends on catalogue cards that are available in each room and that have to be carried round and referred to in front of the exhibits.

Among the treasures of the museum is a beautiful fifteenth-century French statue of St Maurice, which has been placed half-way up the stairs. The youthful saint sits in full armour on a proud horse, his visa up and his hand raised, a faint look of enquiry on his face. At the top of the stairs, the current of people draws one inevitably towards the room containing the series of tapestries known as The Lady and the Unicorn. These are the crown of the museum's collection, and for once the publicity that surrounds them does not lead to disappointment. The tapestries, probably woven in Brussels in the late fifteenth century for Jean Le Viste, exceed expectation. There are five of them illustrating the five senses, each with the lady and the unicorn at the centre, and a sixth in which the lady, watched by the unicorn, hands over a casket of jewels to her attendant at the opening of an ornate tent whose top is embroidered with the words '*A mon seul désir*'. The precise meaning of the allegories can be debated, but their beauty is beyond dispute. It is evident not merely in the central figures but in the exquisite detail of the sharp-eyed little animals and birds glimpsed among the flowers of the background. For just one example look at the delightful dog that lies with nonchalantly crossed forepaws at the corner of the first tapestry, dedicated to 'sight'.

The supremacy of the Lady and the Unicorn tends to overshadow the museum's other tapestries, but there are several that deserve attention. In room 2 an early sixteenth-century portrayal of wine-making is displayed opposite a pretty *offrande du coeur* from the early fifteenth century. Two rooms further on, as part of the series entitled *La Vie Seigneuriale*, you will find another charming tapestry of a lady played to by musicians while she takes her bath. Elsewhere on the ground floor there is a room of thirteenth-century stained glass. Note particularly the delicate panel opposite the door, depicting the angel's announcement to the shepherds of Christ's birth. Downstairs some Roman fragments are exhibited in the area of the baths, but the main attraction here is the so-called Gallery of Kings. These rugged, highly individual stone heads, which were originally sculpted for Notre-Dame in the early thirteenth century and then torn down during the Revolution, stare at us across the centuries with uncompromising power.

As we emerge from the Musée de Cluny, we are looking straight across at the buildings of the SORBONNE. The university which has given this district its character is among the oldest in Europe. It was already in existence when St Louis's confessor, Robert de Sorbon, established a theological college here in the middle of the thirteenth century that in time became the focus of the whole university. Bigotry rather than impartial enquiry was the hallmark of its early history. In the Hundred Years War its voice was for the English against the French and for the burning of Joan of Arc. There was little sympathy here for anything that challenged the narrowest religious orthodoxy; fire and sword were the approved response. The torture and burning of the Knights Templar was firmly supported, as was the later massacre of the Huguenots. (It was the narrow and intolerant spirit of the early Sorbonne that prompted François I in the sixteenth century to found the nearby COLLÈGE DE FRANCE, which for long enjoyed a more distinguished intellectual reputation than its rival.) In the eighteenth century the Sorbonne continued to proclaim its loyalties by calling for the suppression of the *philosophes*. Fire drives out fire, and in 1792 the university was itself suppressed, to be reopened later by Napoleon under new management. In the wake of the upheavals in 1968 the whole structure of Paris universities was again overhauled, and the Sorbonne ended up with the rather less evocative names of Paris III and Paris IV, just a couple of numbers among the capital's thirteen universities. The drab buildings that we see in the rue des Écoles today, opposite the benign statue of Michel de Montaigne, date from the university's expansion at the end of the nineteenth century.

The church of the Sorbonne is normally closed to the public, but if an exhibition is being held, you might look inside to see the tomb of Richelieu. When his body was exposed here after his death in 1642 there was enthusiastic talk among the populace of throwing it in the Seine, so it was hastily withdrawn. One of the more fervent haters of this devious man was the sister of François de Thou. Richelieu had executed her brother a few months before his own death. According to Jacques Hillairet, she offered a large sum of money for permission to have carved on the cardinal's tomb the words of Martha from St John's Gospel,

The pensive figure of Michel de Montaigne faces the buildings of the Sorbonne on the other side of the rue des Écoles.

'Lord, if thou hadst been here, my brother had not died.' In its combination of irreligious wit and venom, the suggestion has an intellectual style that seems peculiarly Parisian.

The rue Saint-Jacques, which runs up between the Sorbonne and the Collège de France, has managed to escape the sort of tourist attentions that have affected much of the area. It is the street that once carried medieval pilgrims out of Paris on their journey to the shrine of St James in Santiago de Compostela. Those who completed the pilgrimage were then entitled to wear the saint's emblem of the scallop shell, which you may have noticed as a decorative motif in the courtyard of the Musée de Cluny.

Our own pilgrimage stops for the moment at the rue Soufflot in the shadow of the massive structure of the PANTHÉON. It was built as a church to fulfill a vow Louis XV had made when he was ill in 1744. Its architect, commemorated by the name of the street we are standing in, was Germain Soufflot. The poor man was apparently so worried about the foundations of the building, which stands above old Roman clay pits, that he died of anxiety. In fact, he was quite right to be worried, as the present state of the Panthéon demonstrates. The main hall is now

The huge dome of the Panthéon, one of Paris's most unmistakable landmarks.

closed because of subsidence. (An explanatory notice near the entrance points out that this will give visitors – who have paid 23 francs – an important opportunity to observe building works in progress.)

By an unfortunate piece of timing, Soufflot's would-be church was completed in 1789, the year the Revolution began. It was a bad moment for churches, and the Panthéon was soon deflected into its present rôle, that of a secular temple to the nation's great men. Its dedication is inscribed in gilt letters on the architrave: AUX GRANDS HOMMES LA PATRIE RECONNAISSANTE. With its huge cupola and profusion of Corinthian columns, it is undoubtedly an impressive monument. Whether it is much more than that is open to question. Though my guide-book tells me that it is 'one of the capital's most popular sights', I find it difficult to feel even moderately excited about the Panthéon. Its huge size is untouched by any imaginative life. One hundred and ten metres long, it presents the visitor with vast stretches of eyeless blank wall that give no hint of anything but a monumental self-importance. To me the interior is as dull as the outside. From the balcony of the cupola there is a close-up of Saint-Étienne-du-Mont and an excellent view of the great dome of the Val-de-Grâce, but otherwise the building has little to offer. The pale frescos of the life of St Geneviève by Puvis de Chavannes are perhaps the only feminine touch in this tediously masculine place. In spite of the work of reconstruction, you can still get a reasonable view of the most attractive of them, of Geneviève watching over the sleeping city.

After all, it may be that the Panthéon manages to draw such crowds simply because people like to take pictures of it. It photographs well. Snapshots, which flatter its stateliness, kindly disguise its lack of life.

Overshadowed by the bulk of the Panthéon, but far more interesting, is the neighbouring church of SAINT-ÉTIENNE-DU-MONT, whose memorable west façade has no less than three pediments. With its ribbed and fluted columns, its pointed gables, its rose window and its scattering of religious statuary, it can strike one at first as a bizarre jumble; but the whole has an eccentric harmony which excites affection. The mixture of styles reflects the period of the church's construction, which runs from the late fifteenth to the early seventeenth centuries, coinciding with the transition from Gothic to the Renaissance. To the north, Saint-Étienne has a fine, slender bell-tower, completed in 1540, which stands 50 metres high and is topped by an attractive lantern. Notice also, above the main entrance, the relief which depicts the stoning of Stephen – St Étienne – the first Christian martyr. Like the other external decorations, this was badly damaged during the Revolution and restored in the nineteenth century by Victor Baltard, the architect responsible for the old market pavilions of Les Halles.

The interior of the church is light and airy, with an attractive balustrade running between the pillars of the nave and choir, but what immediately claims one's attention is the spectacular rood screen, built between 1521 and 1545. From the doorway it looks for a moment almost as though we have stepped into the courtyard of some Moorish palace. The wings of the rood screen rise up in great swirls of stone tracery on either side of the central arch. It is an effect quite unique among the churches of Paris. Every other rood screen in the city has been removed or demolished. Only this superb example in Saint-Étienne remains. Also of interest in the body of the church are the beautiful pendant, 5.5 metres long, which hangs from the keystone of the vault, and the massive wooden pulpit, built in the mid seventeenth century and supported by the figure of Samson who bears it on his shoulder, his knee resting on a slain lion.

Beyond the rood screen, in the right aisle, you can see on either side of the first chapel a carved epitaph – the one on the left for the philosopher and mathematician Blaise Pascal, the one on the right written by Boileau for the classical dramatist Racine. Both of them are buried here, their ashes resting beneath a pillar of the chapel immediately behind the main altar. The chapel next to their epitaphs is dedicated to St Geneviève, patron saint of Paris. Before the Revolution the shrine containing her bones had been venerated here, but even Geneviève's popularity couldn't save her from a hostility to religion that was growing increasingly fierce. In 1793 an impassioned mob seized her shrine, melted it down and burned the bones in the place de Grève (now the place de l'Hôtel-de-Ville). Oddly enough the church then became a Temple to Filial Piety. What you see in the chapel today is a nineteenth-century shrine surrounding part of the original stone sarcophagus which was discovered after the Revolution.

The high point of a tour of St-Étienne is not in the main part of the church at all. If you go through the Sacristy door, a corridor will take you into the Chapel of the Catechisms, where the arches of the old cloister wall have been set with twelve magnificent stained glass windows. They were put here in the eighteenth century, but the glass itself belongs to the same period as the cloister, the late sixteenth and early seventeenth centuries. It is rare that one gets the chance to examine stained glass of this quality in such detail. Look, for example, at the second window near the entrance. Its somewhat unexciting subject is the idea of the Church as a ship, but this has provided the excuse for a brilliant portrayal of Noah's ark, lined with a splendidly individual collection of animals, including a disdainful camel and a rather apprehensive lion on the right. The panel depicting the brazen serpent is noticeably more pallid than the rest, having been made with ordinary coloured glass instead of by the process of enamelling that accounts for the vividness of the others. Even so, it is a marvellous piece of work. The image of the great yellow serpent with its enormous jaws, poised from the fork of a gaunt, leafless tree, is unforgettable. All these windows are a delight to look at. The most famous of them depicts Christ as the mystic wine-press, his body spouting blood in the centre of the panel. But if I had to choose one part of the whole display, it would be the group of little domestic scenes on the left of the final window: the figure baking bread at the top, the cutting-up of the calf just below, and beside this, best of all, the charming vignette of the dog, with eager, alert face, jumping up to get his muzzle into the tub. Altogether this line of cloister windows strikes me as one of the most undervalued sights in Paris.

Standing outside Saint-Étienne-du-Mont, we are on the edge of the distinctive *quartier* centred on the place de la Contrescarpe, where 450 years ago Rabelais used to visit the cabaret of the Pomme de Pin. (The inscription that places this at number 1 is misleading; the cabaret was actually on the corner of the rue Blainville and the rue Mouffetard.) In spite of recent moves up-market, this secluded square, with its two trees and its two street lamps, still retains a faintly provincial quality. The bohemians are being edged out, the down and outs who used to camp under the trees are being shuffled off to remoter pastures, location hunters for advertising agencies have begun to exploit its potential; but there remains something obstinately and appealingly ragged about the place.

Time will no doubt continue to change the place de la Contrescarpe for the worse. Even the disreputable old rue Mouffetard is beginning to brush itself down and look to the tourist trade. There are still one or two of the old-style hotels with a card in the office window giving the address of the nearest municipal showers in the rue Lacépède or a yellowing note pinned permanently to the door with the curt message *Complet – Ne pas déranger*, but these are relics of a way of life that has almost disappeared. New bars, restaurants and brasseries are opening alongside fashionable crêperies; hairdressing salons spring to life behind acres of plate glass; shabby hotel rooms at the top of dimly-lit stone staircases are reborn as desirable apartments. But although the character of the rue Mouffetard is changing, it is still a vital, entertaining place with echoes of a distant past in the old signs on some of the houses. At number 69 a fine oak tree is carved above the doorway, and further on, at number 122, there is an attractive little polychrome image of two figures drawing water from a well – '*A la bonne source*'. Part of the way down we can glance to the right into the rue du Pot-de-Fer, which was the scene of the opening of George Orwell's *Down and Out in Paris and London*. He lived at number 6 in the spring of 1928, long before the street had acquired its present glossily tiled exteriors. Given the record of chronic hunger that Orwell's book presents, it is ironic that number 6, like so many other buildings in the district, has now become a restaurant. Along this half of the rue Mouffetard we run into the colourful street market, overflowing into the place Monge, that does more than anything else to preserve a memory of the street's original character.

At the bottom of the rue Mouffetard, on the left, is the unusual church of SAINT-MÉDARD, whose construction spanned the fifteenth to the seventeenth centuries. Its interest today derives chiefly from the antics of the so-called '*convulsionnaires de Saint-Médard*'. From the rue Daubenton, you can see in the wall the outline of two doorways. The one on the left led to the little cemetery where the *convulsionnaires* held their meetings. The whole business started when a Jansenist deacon, a man of saintly life, much given to mortification of the flesh, died here in 1727. He was buried under a black marble slab which at once became a focus for gatherings of his admirers. Inevitably, there was talk of miracles and the meetings soon began to take on a more extravagant character. The women, in particular, engaged in frenzied excesses, swallowing earth from the deacon's tomb, twisting their breasts, having themselves beaten and trampled on, nailed to crosses and raked with iron combs, anything that a disordered and masochistic fancy could suggest, and all of it undergone with apparent relish. After five years of ever-increasing frenzy, the authorities intervened. The cemetery was closed and a placard nailed to the door: 'By order of the king, God is forbidden to perform miracles in this place.' In the following year, 1733, the doorways were walled up.

The splendid cupola which rises above the buildings to the west of Saint-Médard belongs to the church of the VAL-DE-GRÂCE, built by Anne of Austria in fulfilment of a vow, after she had given birth to the future Louis XIV. To the right of the high altar is the chapel, recently restored thanks to a gift from King Hassan of Morocco, in which her heart was kept from 1666 until the Revolution.

Among other places of interest in this district is the GOBELINS FACTORY. Set up by Colbert in the seventeenth century to produce work for Louis XIV, it simply adopted the name of the area, which was derived from a family of dyers who had lived here since the fifteenth century. It was a feature of the Gobelins that it worked exclusively for the king, and it is still the case that the factory will undertake commissions only from the State. No private work is done here. The business of weaving is carried out by traditional methods which make the process extremely slow. It is quite normal for a single tapestry to take several years to complete. The guided tour round the Gobelins workshops offers anyone who can speak French an instructive glimpse into the meticulous stages by which these tapestries are brought into being.

As you leave the area, you might care to glance at the rather featureless building which stands at 33, rue Croulebarbe, a few yards from where the tour of the Gobelins factory ends. This was Paris's first skyscraper. It's a modest enough affair by the standards of the Tour Montparnasse, but in 1959, when it was built, its 21 floors heralded a transformation of the Paris skyline.

In the neighbourhood of the Gobelins we are out at the fringes of tourist civilization. Few visitors find reason to venture much further into the 13th arrondissement, unless to sample one of the restaurants that have sprung up in the burgeoning Chinatown around the place d'Italie. At this point people tend to make for the nearest Métro and head back to their hotels, but if you can survive a trudge along the tedious boulevard Saint-Marcel, it is worth spending another hour or two in this less frequented part of the city. This boulevard joins the boulevard de l'Hôpital just beside the massive building of the SALPÊTRIÈRE. Founded in the middle of the seventeenth century, the Salpêtrière – its name comes from the gunpowder factory which previously occupied the site – was originally intended as a hospital for the old, the poor and the mad, but to this was added a criminal component which changed its character to that of a prison. In the eighteenth century it became notorious as a place of confinement for errant women of all sorts, including Prévost's Manon Lescaut. Although the hospital was once a byword for the most degraded vice, and the scene of bloody massacres during the Revolution, its more recent history has been distinguished by the research carried out here on insanity. A statue to Philippe Pinel, one of the pioneers of modern psychiatry, stands at the entrance, where a neatly tended garden leads up to the long façade of the hospital.

A short way down the boulevard, on the other side of the road, is a garden of a different sort, which was first opened to the public just a few years before the Salpêtrière. The JARDIN DES PLANTES had been laid out early in the seventeenth century, on the instructions of the royal physician, to provide medicinal herbs, but its scope was later broadened to include the king's menagerie, which was brought from Versailles during the Revolution. Along with the royal collection was an assortment of unusual beasts which had hitherto been trailed around the streets of Paris to be viewed at side-shows. The descendants of these animals came to a sad end at the time of the siege of Paris by the Prussians in 1870 to

1871. For a famished populace the temptation of even the most outlandish sort of steak was too much. E. V. Lucas quotes a contemporary resident who notes that the average price of meat was about 7 francs a pound, though kangaroo had been sold for 12 francs.

Yesterday I dined with the correspondent of a London paper. He had managed to get a large piece of mufflon, an animal which is, I believe, found nowhere but in Corsica. I can only describe it by saying that it tasted of mufflon, and nothing else.

The garden is laid out in neat parterres of flowers at the end of which is a statue to the eighteenth-century naturalist Buffon. Along the sides are heavy phalanxes of plane trees. In summer, especially, it is an agreeable spot, but somehow not quite the kind of thing for which most people go to Paris. Apart from the zoo, its attractions include a museum of Natural History, an ancient Robinia, reputed to be the oldest tree in France, and a section of a two-thousand-year-old sequoia tree from California. This is marked with plaques which indicate the stage of the tree's growth at various points in human history. Strange to reflect that it had already been alive a hundred years by the time the ashes fell on Pompeii.

The naturalist Buffon sitting in state in the Jardin des Plantes. This was founded in 1626 by Guy de la Brosse as a physic garden, but was greatly enlarged by Buffon.

If we leave the Jardin des Plantes by the exit near the menagerie, we can cross straight over to the far side of the quai Saint-Bernard, which has now been turned into an open-air museum of modern sculpture. A variety of pieces have been strung out along the edge of the Seine to take their chances in a rough world and to be enjoyed for as long as they survive. A few, like Nicolas Schoffer's *Chronos 10*, with its metal discs quivering in the wind, have proved irresistible to graffiti artists, but on the whole the experiment seems to be working. For half an hour we can sit among the sculptures and watch the barges chugging past the tip of the Île Saint-Louis.

In earlier times the quai Saint-Bernard offered the spectator a quite different sort of entertainment. It is hard to imagine that swimming in the Seine was ever much fun, especially before the city was blessed with a modern sewage system, but in the seventeenth century this was Paris's prime bathing spot. Since the swimmers were usually naked, the pastime was a source of continuing dismay to moralists and led to the establishment of enclosed baths by 1700.

Today the site is overlooked by the INSTITUT DU MONDE ARABE, whose futuristic building was opened on the corner of this quay in 1987. Designed by Jean Nouvel, it has the sort of ultra-modernity that makes one turn to the Pompidou Centre with a sense of looking back into the past. Both façades of the institute are heat and light sensitive, with computer-operated shutters which close like those of a camera when the sun gets too intense. Inside, glass lifts take you up to the museum on the seventh floor through a web of steel and chrome. The exhibits, among them some superb Persian carpets from the sixteenth century, are interesting enough in their own right, but for most visitors it is probably the building itself that leaves the deepest impression. One tends to remember the display cabinets, suspended by wires in mid-air, long after what they displayed has slipped from the mind.

Twice a year the passers-by along this stretch of the quay would in earlier times have witnessed the gloomy sight of long files of convicts, linked by an iron chain around the neck, setting out on foot for the galleys that awaited them in the French ports. These wretched creatures were kept until their departure at the Château de la Tournelle, just beyond the present site of the institute, and then marched across France to their destination in conditions of horrible cruelty. Civilization progresses; today the quai de la Tournelle is known chiefly as the address of the Restaurant de la Tour d'Argent. On reflection, however, that is perhaps a doubtful proof. If you had asked a courtier of Henri IV what he associated with the quai de la Tournelle, he might well have referred you to an excellent restaurant called the Tour d'Argent. Founded in 1582 and famous for its *caneton pressé*, it is also credited with introducing the use of the fork to Parisian society. Adjoining the restaurant is a little Musée de la Table.

We are now back on what most visitors to Paris will recognize as familiar territory. A left turn takes us on to the boulevard Saint-Germain a few yards from the place Maubert. The square, which is now little more than a hiccup in the boulevard, has a cheerful market three mornings a week, spread out under the

A bronze trio in the Jardin des Plantes.

Jean Nouvel's innovative Institut du Monde Arabe on the corner of the quai Saint-Bernard. The institute was set up to further cultural relations between France and various Arab nations.

trees. Food is attractively displayed everywhere in Paris, but here the vegetables, fruit and cheese are also good value. The square's past has a more sombre character. From the sixteenth to the eighteenth centuries it was a place of public execution. To the surprise of the crowd, at least one of these sordid episodes had a happy ending, when a pair of domestic servants were hanged in 1528 for the murder of their master. After swinging from the gallows for half an hour, one of them turned out to be still alive. He was quick-witted enough to protest that he had indeed been dead, but that a timely prayer to the Virgin just before his execution must have brought him back to life. The story gained enough credence to win him a pardon from François I and a new investigation of the murder. Sure enough, it was discovered that the murder had been done by the victim's wife – cold comfort for the other servant, who had been hanged for the same crime.

The Carmelite convent in which the survivor was allowed to recover gave its name to the neighbouring rue des Carmes, where a taste for such entertainments might lead one to the POLICE MUSEUM at number 1bis just off the edge of the place Maubert. Created by Louis Lépine in 1901, the museum was moved here from the quai des Orfèvres a few years ago. It is only open on Wednesday and Thursday afternoons, but for anyone interested in the murkier underside of the city's history there is plenty here to repay a visit. Apart from the usual display of weapons used for various crimes, along with models of the guillotine and the estrapade, there are also documents relating to a number of the city's more notorious criminals. The Marquise de Brinvilliers, for example, has a whole case to herself. Particularly interesting is a model of the 'machine infernale' designed by Fieschi for the assassination of Louis-Philippe. With its line of pipes it looks like some exotic musical instrument, but it in fact managed to kill nineteen people – pretty well everyone in the vicinity except the intended victim.

The construction of the boulevard Saint-Germain in the middle of the nineteenth century cut through a network of ancient streets, remnants of which can still be found between the place Maubert and the Seine. The rue Galande, which was once part of the main road that led out of Paris towards Lyon and Rome, is one of the oldest of them. In the bottom half of the street, just beyond the rue du Fouarre, you will find number 42. It is an ugly cinema now, much scrawled over with graffiti, but above the door is a charming stone relief from the fourteenth century which depicts St Julien and his wife ferrying Christ across the river to a chapel on the left-hand side. This is the oldest house sign in Paris, mentioned in the city records of 1380. It is true, of course, that plenty of other monuments in plenty of other cities have survived as long and longer, but the modesty of this little carving gives it a particular hold on the imagination. For 600 years people have been passing it by, quite casually, at just this spot. No doubt more than one of the crowd who were pressing on to witness the miraculous execution in 1528 must have glanced up at it as they headed for the place Maubert.

At the edge of these streets is the church of SAINT-JULIEN-LE-PAUVRE, near the end of the rue Galande. It is innocent of any special claim to the tourist's attention, and yet in its simplicity and its aged dignity it can hardly fail to inspire affection. As you go through the door, you are entering the church that was used by St Thomas Aquinas, Dante, Petrarch, Rabelais and François Villon. One of the oldest churches in Paris, dating back in parts to the twelfth century, it must also be one of the least adorned. The screen of icons which separates the choir from the nave was set there in 1901 by the Catholic Melchites to whom the church has belonged since 1889.

There are other streets in this engaging quarter that you will want to see. The rue de la Bûcherie, for example, in which an attempt has been made to reincarnate Sylvia Beach's 'Shakespeare and Company', contains a number of interesting old buildings, including the house at number 16 where the eighteenth-century writer Restif de la Bretonne died in 1806. But when you have wandered to and fro, come back to end your walk in the little square René-Viviani

beside the church. At the entrance, supported by concrete stanchions, is another ancient Robinia tree, said to have been planted by the botanist Robin himself in 1601. If you stroll round it towards the front of the garden, you can sit down and look out across the Seine at a view of Notre-Dame that is reward enough for even the longest journey.

The oldest house-sign in Paris. St Julien and his wife ferry Christ across a river.

6
The Marais

....

THE CENTRE GEORGES POMPIDOU *to* PÈRE LACHAISE

The word *marais* hardly suggests a tempting region of the city. It means 'marsh', and this is exactly what the district to the east of Paris used to be. Even when Philippe-Auguste's wall brought it within the city boundaries in the twelfth century, it was still largely uninhabitable. By this time, however, it had been acquired by the Knights Templar, who went on to drain it and later established their headquarters here. In spite of this, it remained on the sidelines until Henri IV decreed the building of the place Royale (later to become the place des Vosges). At the beginning of the seventeenth century Paris still had no open square that was suitable for grand public occasions. The creation of the place Royale shifted the whole focus of the city to the east and provided a catalyst for the development of the rest of the area. Imposing hôtels sprang up along the neighbouring streets, and the heavy carriages of the nobility lumbered through the *portes-cochères*. The life of the *grand siècle* was underway. This was the world of Richelieu and Mme de Sévigné, of the courtiers, prelates and courtesans whose endless intrigues and changing fortunes shaped the political and social life of the period. Having escaped a massive scheme for its renovation in the early years of this century, the Marais was rapidly crumbling into decline until the writer André Malraux, during his time as de Gaulle's Minister of Culture, set about reversing the process. Thanks largely to him, it has been preserved for us as one of the most fascinating and complex regions of the city.

We can approach the Marais from the direction of the TOUR SAINT-JACQUES, where once the pilgrims began their long journey from Paris to the shrine of Santiago de Compostela in Spain. The tower, which is all that remains of the church of Saint-Jacques-la-Boucherie, was built in the early sixteenth century and is now used by the meteorological service – appropriately enough, since it was here that Pascal carried out his experiments on barometric pressure in the middle of the seventeenth century. A statue of him, clothed in elaborate marble draperies, stands under the arch at the base of the tower.

OPPOSITE *Niki de Saint Phalle's exuberant fountains beside the Pompidou Centre.*

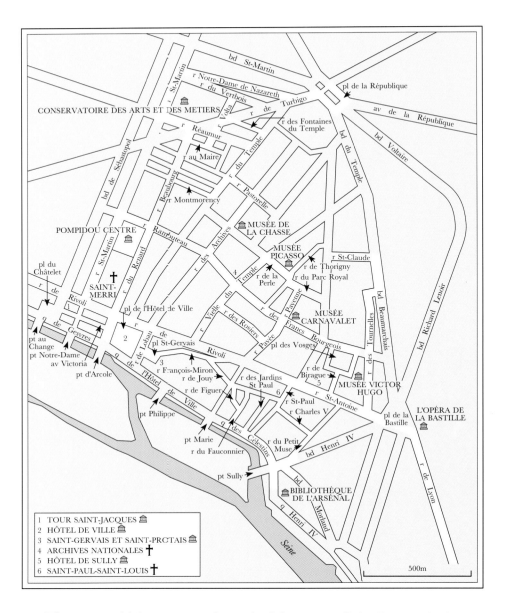

The following labels appear on the map:

bd St-Martin

r Notre-Dame de Nazareth

r du Vertbois

pl de la République

CONSERVATOIRE DES ARTS ET DES METIERS

r de Turbigo

av de la République

Réaumur

r des Fontaines du Temple

bd du Temple

bd Voltaire

r au Maire

r du Temple

bd de Sébastopol

r Pastorelle

r Montmorency

r des Archives

MUSÉE DE LA CHASSE

POMPIDOU CENTRE

Rambuteau

r St-Martin

MUSÉE PICASSO

r St-Claude

r de Thorigny

r du Parc Royal

pl du Châtelet

r du Renard

r du Temple

r de la Perle

bd Beaumarchais

r de Rivoli

SAINT-MERRI

pl de l'Hôtel de Ville

Vielle du Temple

r des Rosiers

r Pavée

MUSÉE CARNAVALET

r des Tournelles

bd Richard Lenoir

r de Gesvres

pt au Change

pt Notre-Dame

av Victoria

pt d'Arcole

r de Lobau

pl St-Gervais

r Rivoli

r des Francs Bourgeois

pl des Vosges

r de Birague

MUSÉE VICTOR HUGO

L'OPÉRA DE LA BASTILLE

q de l'Hôtel de Ville

r François-Miron

r de Jouy

r de Figuer

r des Jardins St Paul

r St-Antoine

r St-Paul

r Charles V

pl de la Bastille

pt Philippe

pt Marie

q des Célestins

r du Petit Musc

bd Henri IV

r du Fauconnier

pt Sully

bd Henri IV

q Henri IV

q Morland

BIBLIOTHÈQUE DE L'ARSÉNAL

r de Lyon

Seine

500m

1 TOUR SAINT-JACQUES

2 HÔTEL DE VILLE

3 SAINT-GERVAIS ET SAINT-PROTAIS

4 ARCHIVES NATIONALES

5 HÔTEL DE SULLY

6 SAINT-PAUL-SAINT-LOUIS

THE MARAIS

The street which runs past the end of the square Saint-Jacques is the old Roman road to the north, the rue Saint-Martin. This section of it is now a pedestrian precinct, lined with a number of pleasant café–restaurants. Just beyond the church of SAINT-MERRI, the street opens into a wide piazza that slopes down to the Centre National d'Art et de Culture Georges-Pompidou. Squatting at the edge of the city's oldest district, the POMPIDOU CENTRE could scarcely present a greater contrast. For well over a decade now, its bulging mass of pipes and tubes has excited horror and admiration but rarely indifference. The work of the British architect Sir Richard Rogers and the Italian Renzo Piano, it was constructed between 1972 and 1977 at the urging of President Pompidou, who expanded the original scheme of using the site for a public library. Whatever one may think of it – and personally I have grown rather fond of it, an increasingly shabby Caliban among the sedate buildings usually favoured by officialdom – it has been undeniably successful in drawing the crowds, and this continues to be the case long after its novelty value has worn off.

One reason for its success is apparent as soon as you step into the piazza. This is a place where people come to enjoy themselves. The fire-eaters, mime artists, organ grinders, conjurors and comedians attract a crowd that drifts quite naturally from the entertainments of the piazza to the entertainments of the cultural centre and back again. The centre itself is the opposite of claustrophobic, and it practises none of the cultural intimidation that galleries sometimes go in for. The bulk of the permanent collection is housed on the fourth floor, which you reach by an escalator that zig-zags up the side of the building inside a transparent cylinder. Parts of it are beginning to look a bit grimy now, but the journey up is still fun. From the terrace on the fourth floor there is a stirring view across Paris. Saint-Eustache, in particular, stands out well, as do the church and terraces of Sacré-Coeur, which perhaps look better from here than from any other perspective. (To see Notre-Dame you must go up to the café on the fifth floor, where the view again is wonderful, but the café itself rather less than wonderful.)

Inside the gallery, what strikes one immediately is the number of French people there, even at the height of the tourist season. It is a rare achievement for a gallery of this kind to attract so much native support. But it is an unusual gallery –

Sonia Delaunay, Contrastes simultanes, *1912*.

light, spacious, comfortable. To me it seems an altogether admirable setting in which to look at paintings like Matisse's *Goldfish Bowl*, Emil Nolde's *Still Life with Dancers*, Georges Braque's *The Duo*, Delaunay's hectic visions of the Eiffel Tower and Delvaux's mysterious *The Acropolis*. Replace them with what names you will – the experience is guaranteed to be a pleasure.

Before you leave, make sure you have a look at Jean Tinguely's huge mobile downstairs, *L'enfer, un petit début* (1984). Every fifteen minutes the whole assembly jerks into life – hammers bang, tin cans clatter, Mickey Mouse bobs up and down, a moose's head swings round, a bowl of ferns rotates, in every direction scraps of junk are briefly resurrected. Whether you choose to take it seriously or not, it is a memorable performance.

One display that makes no claim at all to seriousness is the pool of fountains at the south side of the Pompidou Centre. From one of the adjacent café tables you can watch water spouting from red lips, red hearts, snakes' mouths, skulls, elephant trunks and assorted monsters. It's a fountain playground that makes a cheerful complement to the pleasures of the piazza and the gallery.

Before returning to the main business of our walk, we must carry on for a few yards up the rue Saint-Martin until a sign directs us to the *Horloge à Automate*. This extravagant clock, a couple of years younger than the Pompidou Centre, is set against the wall of an unsightly pink building in the rue Bernard-de-Clairvaux. It presents an engaging allegory of the Defence of Time. Try to get here on the hour, preferably at midday, 6 p.m. or 10 p.m., when all its figures are in action at once. As the hour sounds in doom-like tones, the dragon (earth), the crab (sea) and the bird (air) spring threateningly to life – even the dragon's belly heaves in anticipation of the fight. The Defender of Time, a strange brazen warrior standing on a rocky outcrop of metal, lunges at each of them in turn to the sound of menacing music which carries a hint of waves, winds and tremors of the earth. When Time has been defended for another span, the sound dies and the figures subside. The concept of defending Time from the assaults of Nature seems slightly odd to me, since it would be more usual to think of Time as the aggressor; but perhaps in this case it is Time as a measure of human achievement that is under attack. Either way, the result is impressive, particularly, I think, at 10 p.m., when the eeriness of the display is accentuated by the uncertain light. The brass clock, which weighs a tonne, was made by Jacques Monestier between 1975 and 1979.

After these two excursions into the Paris of the 1970s, we can walk back to the place de l'Hôtel-de-Ville and turn our faces towards the Marais. Like many other buildings in the city centre, the old HÔTEL DE VILLE was fired by the Commune in 1871 and what we see today is a painstaking and rather lifeless reconstruction of it. The square itself was the scene of fierce fighting towards the end of the German Occupation, but on the whole its twentieth-century aspect belies its violent past. It is now a large, dead, paved area relieved only by a prodigious number of street lamps. Formerly called the place de Grève, it used to be about half its present size and was for 500 years, from the early fourteenth century, the city's main place of execution. Hanging, burning, beheading, breaking on the wheel

– all could be relied on to pack the surrounding houses and rooftops with eager spectators. Inevitably, the more gruesome displays drew the largest crowds. While Damiens was having his flesh pulled off by pincers and then being torn apart alive for his attempt on the life of Louis XV, Casanova was at one of the windows of the square, observing the rapt attention that his female companions gave to the spectacle. At other times the place de Grève was the gathering place for unemployed workers – hence the phrase *faire la grève*, to be on strike.

Behind the building of the Hôtel de Ville is the little place Saint-Gervais, whose seventeenth-century church of SAINT-GERVAIS-SAINT-PROTAIS presents a somewhat dingy façade, which boasts an eclectic mixture of Doric, Ionic and Corinthian capitals. Inside, the second chapel in the right aisle contains an uninspired memorial to the 50 people killed when a German bomb landed on the church on Good Friday 1918.

Alongside the church, the rue François-Miron, named after a magistrate in the time of Henri IV, leads into the heart of the Marais. Among the oldest buildings here are numbers 11 and 13, on the corner of the rue Cloche-Perce, both dating from the fifteenth century. Their ground floors are now occupied by a pretty restaurant and a shop selling elegant *japonaiserie*. Also of note in this street is the Hôtel de Beauvais at number 68, built in the seventeenth century for Pierre de Beauvais and his wife, Catherine Bellier. The hôtel is decorated by a number of images of ram's heads, which make a visual pun on Catherine's name, *bélier* meaning ram. Indeed, the house owed more to the one-eyed Catherine than it did to her husband, since it was built as a reward for her intimate services to Queen Anne of Austria, whose lady-in-waiting she had been, and for her equally intimate services to the queen's son, the future Louis XIV. Aging and ugly but of an amorous disposition, Cateau la Borgnesse, as she was called, had undertaken the delicate task of initiating the sixteen-year-old Louis into manhood. When she brought back a favourable report, the Queen's delight was such that Cateau could retire comfortably on the proceeds. Later occupants of the house included Queen Christina of Sweden and, for a few months in 1763, the young Mozart. At seven years of age he had already done the rounds of several European courts, relentlessly promoted by his father Leopold, but the Paris of Louis XV opened new and extravagant scenes. To stand behind the king's table at Versailles, to be caressed by Mme de Pompadour, to play before the Prince de Conti – these were landmarks even in the progress of a prodigy.

Older than the Hôtel de Beauvais, indeed one of the oldest mansions in Paris, is the Hôtel de Sens in the nearby rue du Figuier. A product of the late fifteenth century, this medieval building, with its rounded turrets and decorated gables, might seem to be redolent of the days of immured princesses, but it was in fact built for the archbishops of Sens. In 1605 it became the temporary home of Henri IV's wife Marguerite de Valois, la reine Margot. For the previous eighteen years she had been banished to the country in an attempt to check the scandal that attended her remarkably dissolute life-style. (She had started collecting lovers at the early age of 11.) If it was felt that the religious associations of the house would

combine with her advancing years and gross obesity to give her inclinations a more spiritual turn, there had been a sad miscalculation. The 52-year-old queen, bald and heavily powdered, lost no time in settling again to the pleasures of the capital. Alas, when she sought to replace the Comte de Vermond, who was twenty at the time, with a younger and more vigorous suitor, the eighteen-year-old son of a carpenter, the count took offence and killed his rival on the doorstep of the Hôtel de Sens just as the latter was returning from church with his mistress. Beside herself with rage and grief, Margot had the count beheaded at the door of the hôtel two days later. After that the place was not the same. The Hôtel de Sens reverted to its archbishops and Margot left for the other side of Paris.

From the hôtel it is only a few yards to the quai des Célestins, where we can look across to the shapely curve of the Île Saint-Louis (pp. 24–8), with its line of tall poplar trees. In times of danger a huge chain was stretched across the river at this point to prevent the incursions of enemy ships. A plaque on the corner of the rue des Jardins-Saint-Paul records that it was in this street that François Rabelais died on 9 April, 1553.

At the end of the quai des Célestins you might pause a moment in the square Henri-Galli, an island of peace at the centre of several roaring lines of traffic. Wander over to the south-east corner and you will find there, surrounded by shrubs and flowers, a few surviving stones from the old fortress of the Bastille. Across the road from here is the ARSENAL LIBRARY, housed in the remains of the great mansion built for Henri IV's minister, the Duc de Sully, at the end of the sixteenth century. Among its treasures is a fascinating range of documents which includes such details as we have about the Man in the Iron Mask.

Another set of papers in the Arsenal library relates to what is known as the *affaire des poisons* at the centre of which was a former midwife called la Voisin who

OPPOSITE *The formal display in the courtyard of the fifteenth-century Hôtel de Sens.*

LEFT *Some of the remains of the once-formidable Bastille have been placed in the square Henri-Galli.*

had begun by selling love potions and then graduated to poisons. After her arrest she began to implicate among her clients so many members of the court that the whole business was brought to a swift and satisfactory conclusion by having her burned at the stake before she could say any more. But this was only the continuation of a saga that had begun some years earlier in 1651 when the newly married Marquise de Brinvilliers came to live here in the Marais. If you walk up to 12 rue Charles-V, you can see the substantial hôtel, built some three decades earlier, into which she moved. The years that followed ensured her place as one of the most notorious women in French history.

Behind it all was the desire to inherit her family's wealth, but first the intervening members of the family had to be dealt with. After experimenting with various poisons concocted by herself and her lover, which in the course of her charitable work at the Hôtel Dieu she was able to try out on the hospital inmates, she began with her father, who succumbed at the tenth attempt. In a murderous sequence that is now irresistibly reminiscent of *Kind Hearts and Coronets*, she proceeded from father to elder brother, to sister-in-law, to younger brother, botched the attempt on her sister (who was a Carmelite nun) and then moved on to her husband – though at this point her lover was frantically administering antidotes for fear that if she succeeded in dispatching her husband he might himself be elected as a replacement. It was the lover's death and the subsequent discovery of a casket of incriminating papers that brought everything to light. The Marquise de Brinvilliers fled abroad but was finally trapped and brought back to France to be tortured, beheaded and burned. Along with all the rest, Mme de Sévigné watched her end. What gave the event a peculiar piquancy was the religious conversion Mme de Brinvilliers had undergone shortly before, which expressed itself in an extreme piety. On the day after the burning, notes Mme de Sévigné, the populace were sifting through the ashes in search of bones, believing her to have been a saint. A less spiritual legacy was the rash of poisonings which swept the city in the later years of the century.

From the end of the rue Charles-V we can walk up to the rue Saint-Antoine. On our left is the church of SAINT-PAUL-SAINT-LOUIS, on our right, across the road, the majestic Hôtel de Sully. Built for the Jesuits in the 1630s, the church was soon a fashionable place of worship for the aristocratic population of the neighbourhood, where Mme de Sévigné came to listen to the preaching of Louis Bourdaloue. The Jesuit influence is immediately apparent in the decorative elaboration of the interior, with its ornamented vaulting and forest of Corinthian capitals. The two stoups, one on each side of the entrance, are a later addition. Victor Hugo, who was living at the time in the place des Vosges, presented them to the church to mark the christening of his first son.

The HÔTEL DE SULLY was built a decade or so before the church, probably to the designs of Jean Androuet du Cerceau. As you enter the fine courtyard, you have ahead of you the figures of Autumn and Winter, carved between the first-floor windows, with corresponding figures of Air, Fire, Earth and Water, on the side wings. Spring and Summer are on the other side of the central wing, facing

the Orangerie across another pretty courtyard. Today the building houses the office of historic monuments, but the apparatus of bureaucracy is discreetly concealed from public view. The handsomely decorated interior of the hôtel can be seen by guided tour.

At the side of the Orangerie is a small doorway that leads into a corner of the place des Vosges. As you glance through it, you can perhaps imagine the eccentric ghost of the original Duc de Sully, an old man as he was by this time but dressed in the long-forgotten fashions of his youth, dripping with jewels, parading around the arcades of the great square with one of the dubious female companions provided by his secretary. In another part of the hôtel his wife is occupied according to her taste; the duke has already supplied her with the month's allowance, doling it out in his usual fashion – so much for the house, so much for herself, so much for her lovers. These last caused him little distress, but he objected to bumping into them on the stairs. Accordingly, he arranged a separate staircase for them, leading to his wife's apartments.

As we continue down this section of the rue Saint-Antoine towards the Bastille, we are walking along the old jousting field where Henri II was killed in

A courtyard of the early seventeenth-century Hôtel de Sully with relief carvings of Spring and Summer above the doorway.

1559, accidentally pierced through the eye by the lance of Count Montgomery, the captain of his guard. The appearance of things at the end of the street has changed dramatically over the years, not least over the past five. The mighty fortress that once stood here was built towards the end of the fourteenth century. Under Richelieu it became a high-class prison. There was no nonsense about courts of justice; its inmates, usually people who had given some offence to the king, were merely received by the Governor with a *lettre de cachet* requesting that they be detained until further orders. Though the regime was not harsh – indeed, wealthier residents could make it positively luxurious – life behind walls 11 metres high and 3 metres thick can never have been ideal. Voltaire, Vanbrugh and de Sade all spent time here, but unlike the Man in the Iron Mask (actually it was made of velvet, according to the records), they survived to see the outside world again. When the Bastille was finally stormed by the mob on 14 July, 1789, it had already long outlived its usefulness, but it remained a potent symbol of oppression. A line of brown stones in the place de la Bastille now marks its site.

If Napoleon had had his way, and for once I wish he had, the centre of the square would today be occupied by a splendid bronze elephant cast from captured cannon and spouting water from its trunk. As it is, we have the Colonne de Juillet, set up to commemorate those killed in the street fighting of 1830 which put an end to the Bourbon dynasty. Among the fallen was Victor Hugo's Gavroche, the engaging urchin of *Les Misérables*.

The one thing that has so far not been mentioned is, of course, precisely what every visitor first sees on entering the square. The new BASTILLE OPERA HOUSE is the most recent in a long line of buildings by which France's rulers have sought to leave their imprint on the nation's capital. Completed at huge expense in 1989, this one has come in for more than the usual share of vilification – much of it merely an expression of prejudice. Given the constraints of putting any modern building of this size on this site, it seems to me remarkably successful. Photos – at least those that I have seen – tend to do it less than justice. The imaginative blend of curves and straight lines has produced a façade that manages to be good-looking without being absurdly intrusive. In striking contrast to Garnier's opera house (pp. 54–5), the interior has been designed by the Canadian architect Carlos Ott with a clear sense of practical requirements. The acoustics of the auditorium are superb, and the seating, in black velvet rather than the traditional red, can accommodate well over 2500 people. The seats are themselves an example of the concern that has gone into planning the acoustics. They have been so designed that when the auditorium is empty they give back the same degree of sound as when it is full, so that effects can be accurately gauged during rehearsal. Other refinements range from the basement amphitheatre with a projection screen for late arrivals to the panoramic bar which will be opening on the seventh floor. If François Mitterand wishes to leave an architectural monument behind him, he could have done much worse.

Part of the aim of the whole venture has been to revitalize an area that was beginning to look increasingly shabby. New cafés and brighter, more salubrious shops suggest that this is already coming to pass, although whether the locals are likely to welcome such changes is more doubtful. The streets which radiate out to the east of the place de la Bastille belong to an area that has strong working-class traditions. The rue du Faubourg-Saint-Antoine was, and to a large extent still is, the preserve of the furniture-makers. It was also the breeding ground of Revolution. (Dickens was making an accurate judgement when he placed Defarge's wine-shop in this district in *A Tale of Two Cities*.) A revolution without a barricade across the rue du Faubourg-Saint-Antoine would have been unthinkable throughout the nineteenth century. But today the street has the unmistakable bloom of prosperity. There is little impulse to revolt here. Far too much is at stake among these elegant premises, where expensive furniture is purveyed to the wealthy middle classes. Even the rue de Lappe, which still retains something of its old *louche* dilapidation, is showing glimpses of plate glass and chromium, as new cocktail bars and galleries come into being. Perhaps the locals themselves are beginning to change.

It was in the house on the corner of the place de la Bastille, at number 1, that Giuseppe Fieschi prepared his '*machine infernale*', the home-made, multi-barrelled gun with which he proposed to blast Louis-Philippe into a better life in July 1835. As it turned out, the plot misfired and Fieschi ended up on the scaffold in the place Saint-Jacques.

To the south, the rue de Lyon leads straight down from the place de la Bastille to the Gare de Lyon. The station hardly warrants a special pilgrimage, but if ever you find yourself here, *en route* for the sun, its restaurant, 'Le Train Bleu', offers a wonderful *fin-de-siècle* setting for your lunch. As you look out over the tracks that disappear towards the south of France, you can spend a happy moment thinking of other travellers whose fate has consigned them for lunch to one of London's railway stations.

As we turn back from the place de la Bastille into the Marais, we can stroll along the stately rue des Tournelles, whose entrance is marked by a statue of Beaumarchais. It was in the seventeenth-century house at number 36, its doorway surmounted by a battered stone head, that Ninon de Lenclos spent most of the last 40 years of her life. She stands out from the self-seeking, somewhat sordid, somewhat ruthless chronicles of the Marais as a refreshingly attractive figure. Her early life as a courtesan was so scandalous that she was for a time confined by order of the queen to the prison of the Madelonettes; but the word courtesan is misleading, for her affairs with many of the greatest names in France were quite unmercenary. She had wit, intelligence and a gift for friendship which included women as well as men – even Scarron's prudish wife, the future Mme de Maintenon, seems to have had a tender spot for her. In later life she established in this house a renowned literary salon that attracted everyone from Molière to Mme de Sévigné, La Rochefoucauld to La Fontaine. She died here in 1705.

Before we step into the place des Vosges, you might like to make a brief detour to the eighteenth-century Hôtel de Cagliostro at 1, rue Saint-Claude. It was here that the great impostor lived at the height of his fame from 1785–1786.

Caron de Beaumarchais, writer of The Barber of Seville *and* The Marriage of Figaro, *stands at the opening of the rue des Tournelles.*

Joseph Balsamo – the Comte de Cagliostro was a courtesy title he gave himself – arrived in Paris with a European reputation as a healer, alchemist and communer with spirits. He found a credulous population ready to fall at his feet, and the hôtel in the rue Saint-Claude quickly became a focus for eager visitors from the highest reaches of Parisian society who attended his séances here and marvelled at all the paraphernalia of the occult – strange symbols, tranced acolytes, esoteric incantations and obscure predictions. Cagliostro's performance must have been phenomenally effective. He was never convincingly exposed, even though the king chased him out of France. It was left to the pope to find a Christian solution by having him arrested on a charge of practising Freemasonry and imprisoned until his death in 1795.

Your first view of the place des Vosges is something to be savoured. Even the architecture of the surrounding streets will have left you unprepared for this magnificent enclosure. Ideally, you should enter the square under the Pavillon du Roi and walk in opposite the statue of Louis XIII. (Louis himself does not benefit from close inspection. He has one of the silliest expressions on his face of any statue I know. Put up in 1829, this equestrian monument replaces an earlier bronze statue that had been set here in 1639.) The whole experience of the place des Vosges is one of harmony, from the regular patterns of pink brick and white stone to the soothing geometry of the lawns. The atmosphere of this square, as one sits under the trees and watches the four graceful fountains spraying their water into the sunlight, is unlike anything else in Paris. One can't help feeling that the infants who are regularly wheeled through here in their prams must start life with a singular advantage. Even the grass is well tended – and this in Paris, which used to rank anything as a lawn that could boast more than half a dozen blades of grass struggling through the mud.

I can work up little enthusiasm for wandering round with guide-book in hand, checking number 1bis where Mme de Sévigné was born, number 8 where Théophile Gautier wrote *Mademoiselle de Maupin*, number 11 where the great courtesan Marion Delorme lived in the 1640s, number 21 which was Richelieu's hôtel and so on. It's much pleasanter to make for one of the tables of the Brasserie Ma Bourgogne – you will be following in the footsteps of Inspector Maigret – and just enjoy being here. It looks what it is, and what it was once called, the place Royale. From the time of its creation in the early seventeenth century this was the centre of the Marais and the focus of its social life, the scene of duels and rendez-vous, literary salons and political intrigues.

After our halt at the brasserie we shall perhaps not want to do anything too energetic, but it would be a pity to leave the square without visiting the hôtel at number 6 where Victor Hugo lived from 1832 to 1848. The MUSÉE VICTOR HUGO which is now installed here has an interesting range of memorabilia. Apart from Hugo's apartment on the second floor, with its enviable view across the *place*, there are illustrations of his novels by Gustave Brion and Emile Bayard as well as a number of his own dark and menacing pictures. On the walls hang a series of portraits and photographs. Boulanger's portrait of Mme Hugo puts one in mind of Dickens's comment after he had visited the family here in 1847: 'His wife is a handsome woman with flashing black eyes, who looks as if she might poison his breakfast any morning when the humour seized her.' Among the photographs is one of their daughter Adèle, her head leaning wistfully to one side – quite different from the later, harder photograph of her on the opposite wall. Other works to note are the painting of the elderly but still beautiful Juliette Drouet in 1883 and Rodin's powerful bust of Hugo himself in old age.

The rue des Francs-Bourgeois (or Francs-Citoyens, as they became briefly during the Revolution) leads westward out of the place des Vosges and took its name from a poor-house established here in the fourteenth century, whose inmates were exempt from taxes and therefore classified as *francs bourgeois*. It is a street filled with good things. A short way down on the left is the Hôtel Lamoignon. Older than most of the buildings in the Marais, it dates in part from the sixteenth century and now houses a library devoted to the history of Paris. It was here, as a plaque on the side wall informs us, that Alphonse Daudet lived from 1867 to 1876. Next to the hôtel, another plaque draws our attention to traces of the old prison of the *Petite-Force*, where for a time Choderlos de Laclos, the author of *Les liaisons dangereuses*, was held prisoner. The scene of some of the most horrible massacres in September 1792, it was from here that the Princesse de Lamballe was taken out to her brutal death. The prison was finally demolished in the middle of the nineteenth century.

Before we cross over to the Musée Carnavalet, there are a couple of places further down the street that claim our attention. The little MUSÉE KWOK ON at number 41 is devoted to oriental theatre and tends to attract only a sprinkling of visitors even when tourists are thick on the ground elsewhere. The explanatory notices beside exhibits are full of information but don't actually leave one with a very clear sense of what the museum is trying to do. Nevertheless, we are offered a brilliantly colourful display of puppets, costumes, religious robes, banners, dragons' heads and even one complete dragon, stretched full-length across the central exhibition room.

In its way the Kwok On is highly typical of the area we are walking through. There is a general air of slightly exotic connoisseurship about the Marais. Its streets are old and for the most part rather narrow, and its shops, with low fronts and recessed windows, are interspersed with seventeenth-century doorways and private apartments. The shops are individual not just in their appearance, but also in the goods they sell. There is no feeling here of the uniform or the mass produced. The clothes you find in one shop are unlikely to be the same as those in the shop next door. The bars and restaurants have an equally distinctive character. As a whole, the area tends to go in for the old, the quirky and the uncommon, all kept in balance by the presence of solid, substantial seventeenth-century stone.

None more solid than in the walls of the Hôtel des Ambassadeurs de Hollande which we pass in a moment at 47, rue Vieille-du-Temple. It was here that Caron de Beaumarchais wrote *The Marriage of Figaro* in 1778. If we turn left just beyond this hôtel, we shall find ourselves in the rue des Rosiers, heading back towards Carnavalet. The street has no building of special note, but it is of considerable interest as the centre of the Jewish quarter which became a feature of the Marais earlier this century. Kosher pizza, Israeli fast food, a small shop selling Jewish art, and a printer specializing in Hebrew – all of them represent a community that, until the Marais became fashionable again, had more or less made it their own. On Sundays the rue des Rosiers is still the liveliest street in the area.

A visit to the MUSÉE CARNAVALET is one of the delights of a walk through the Marais. The place is packed with an incomparable range of historical exhibits. If only it were slightly easier to find one's way around them, the experience would be one of unmixed enjoyment, but even with the plan handed out at the ticket office there are still problems. This is partly because large sections of the museum are frequently closed, partly, perhaps, because the exhibition space has recently been extended into the neighbouring Hôtel le Pelletier de Saint-Fargeau.

OPPOSITE *A fountain in the place des Vosges, laid out by Henri IV at the beginning of the seventeenth century.*

Giuseppe Canella, La place de la Concorde, *1829.*

Among the most intriguing items in the museum are some images of Paris in the sixteenth century. In room 7, for example, there are a couple of superb Flemish paintings, one of the Cimetière des Innocents, the other depicting the prodigal son among courtesans, with the spires of Paris in the background. In the same room a model of the huddled Île de la Cité shows houses reaching almost to the porch of Notre-Dame. (It's striking to see how many other churches there were at the time within a few yards of the cathedral.) Elsewhere, the museum is well stocked with pictures of Paris from the eighteenth century through to the twentieth. Their interest is only partly a matter of topography – what has changed and what hasn't. More important, perhaps, is the way these images become gradually absorbed into our own perceptions of the city. They invest the commonplace sights of a modern capital with an imaginative richness that links them layer by layer to a world that no longer exists. Once we know them, the experience of standing in the place de l'Hôtel-de-Ville or looking across at the quai de la Tournelle has been subtly changed.

Portraits of Molière, Corneille and La Fontaine can be found in other rooms of the museum, as can a rather different sort of portrait by Jean Huber of Voltaire pulling on his trousers, with an inquisitive dog at his side. Of particular interest is the collection relating to the Revolution. Along with the keys to the Bastille is a model of the fortress carved out of one of its stones. (The contractor responsible for demolishing it made a comfortable income out of this sort of souvenir.) Other relics include Lafayette's sword, Danton's spoon and fork, Robespierre's plate and Saint-Just's pistol. They look much the same as anyone else's sword, spoon, fork etc., but if you are in the right mood they can provide an enjoyable frisson. More expressive is the unflattering series of portraits. Danton, Desmoulins, Robespierre, Marat and Charlotte Corday are all represented here, as well as the icy-looking Dr Guillotin. The new layout of the museum is such that you can find yourself moving almost straight from scenes of the Revolution to the delightful room devoted to literary life in the twentieth century, where exhibits range from the furniture of Marcel Proust to a portrait of Juliette Greco. In all, it is a wonderfully varied museum, sometimes frustrating but packed with interest. And for those, like myself, who have a taste for the byways of Paris's social history, the Carnavalet bookshop is a treasure house.

Quite apart from the museum, the building itself is of great interest. For the last nineteen years of her life, it was the home of Mme de Sévigné. She moved here in 1677, enticed by 'fine air, a fine courtyard, a fine garden, a fine district', and mementoes of her life, including manuscripts of some of the letters and a portrait of her by Robert Nanteuil, are on display inside. She, better than anyone, catches the tone of society life in the heyday of the Marais, passing on vivid accounts of its scandals and dramas to her beloved daughter in Provence. She announces with satisfaction that her rather less beloved son, Charles, has just broken off with Ninon de Lenclos, but the real news is that while seeking consolation with another mistress he had suffered an attack of impotence at the crucial moment and is now out of favour with her as well. Mme de Sévigné finds such episodes hugely amusing:

> The other day, Charles told me of an actor who wanted to get married although he was suffering from a certain somewhat dangerous infection; and his friend said to him, 'Good God, wait till you're cured; otherwise you'll be the death of us all!' This struck me as a pretty piece of wit.

The advice she gives her daughter in the same letter seems eminently characteristic of this attractive woman, and of the world in which she lived:

> But don't delve too deeply into your mind. Reflections are sometimes dark enough to make us die; we must glide a little over the surface of our thoughts, you know.

The Hôtel Carnavalet owes its present appearance to François Mansart, who redesigned it in the middle of the seventeenth century. Antoine Coysevox's statue of Louis XIV, which dominates Mme de Sévigné's 'fine courtyard', is an admirable piece, noteworthy as the only royal statue to escape destruction during the Revolution. By an odd chance it was erected on 14th July 1689, exactly 100

This bronze of Louis XIV posing as a Roman emperor was cast by Coysevox in 1689 and stands in the grounds of the Hôtel Carnevalet.

years before the fall of the Bastille. As you turn back through the entrance, have a look at the figure above the doorway, holding a cornucopia; notice that the feet rest on a stone carved into the form of a carnival mask – yet another of Paris's visual puns. The splendid lions on either side were carved by Jean Goujon.

Just north of the Carnavalet, at 5 rue de Thorigny, is the HÔTEL SALÉ, so called because its construction was financed by the owner's profits as a collector of the salt tax. For anyone with an interest in Picasso, this will require a morning to itself, since it now houses the MUSÉE PICASSO – a vast collection of his works, running through from the earliest canvases, painted at the turn of the century under the influence of Van Gogh and Lautrec, to a work like *Vieil Homme Assis*, painted at the end of 1971 and still rich in colour and life. The range and diversity of the art is stunning. Whether this is the ideal context for it is another question. The claim made by the museum that the hôtel is a particularly appropriate spot for Picasso's work because he himself often lived in similarly historic buildings rings somewhat hollow. But perhaps we should just be grateful for what is on display – both the paintings and the place. The hôtel, which served for a time as the Venetian Embassy, was built in the mid seventeenth century by Jean Boullier. Notice in particular the wrought iron staircase with its motif of an interlaced A and C, the initials of Pierre Aubert, the aging salt king, and his sprightly young wife whose family name was Chastelain. The lovely decoration around the staircase and ceiling is the work of Gaspard Marsy and Martin Desjardins.

From the rue de Thorigny it is only a short step to the HÔTEL DE ROHAN in the rue Vieille-du-Temple, which now houses sections of the NATIONAL ARCHIVES that have overflowed from the neighbouring Hôtel de Soubise. The interior of the hôtel is notable both for the Fable Room, whose panels are decorated with charming scenes from La Fontaine's fables, and also for the more famous *Cabinet des Singes*, decorated by Christophe Huet in 1749–50. Here you may find that the images of little pig-tailed Chinese gambolling in pastoral landscapes rather diminishes your pleasure. If so, consolation is at hand. In a quiet courtyard of the hôtel, with a line of trees and an unkempt lawn edged by rosebushes, you can stand and gaze at Robert Le Lorrain's astonishing relief of the Horses of Apollo. Seen for the first time, this wonderfully dramatic tableau comes upon one quite unexpectedly. Amid the tranquil setting, where today the only sound is likely to be the clicking of typewriters from the surrounding offices, these four horses preserve a fierce, independent power.

The main body of the National Archives is housed next door in the HÔTEL DE SOUBISE. This is probably more often visited by the specialist than the tourist, but the museum upstairs contains some fascinating documents, among them certificates from King Dagobert and Charlemagne, a letter dictated by Joan of Arc, the Edict of Nantes, a letter from the father of Camille Desmoulins addressed to Fouquier-Tinville in favour of his son, the last letter of Marie-Antoinette, and pages recording the verdicts of the deputies on Louis XVI. These are just a sample of the papers on display. As a bonus to your visit, you can also see a couple of seductive pastorals by Boucher downstairs in the Chambre du Prince.

Nearby, in the rue des Archives, is the massive turreted entrance to the four-teenth-century Hôtel de Clisson. This is practically all that remains of the mansion that later passed into the hands of the Guise family, who here laid plans for the Massacre of St Bartholomew.

Further up the rue des Archives, you should try to spare an hour for the MUSÉE DE LA CHASSE. Housed in another attractive seventeenth-century hôtel, built by Mansart, this is a real curiosity. Don't be put off by the name – you are not letting yourself in for three floors of moose heads and stuffed animals. Only one room in the whole place is entirely given over to this sort of trophy, and even here the exhibits are far from ordinary – along with the usual leopards and lions, there are sad gorillas, a rhinoceros, and a huge crocodile with eyes squeezed close together at the top of its head, looking like a grim messenger from prehistory. The major part of the museum is concerned with the impetus that hunting has given to art, and the result is an absorbing and idiosyncratic collection that ranges from fourteenth-century Japanese paintings to exquisitely inlaid arquebuses. Among the highlights is a lovely fifteenth-century sculpture of the vision of St Hubert, in which the deer with the crucifix between its horns looks much more startled than the saint. Elsewhere there are fine Flemish tapestries, uncommon paintings, and some extraordinary hunting implements – one monstrous object from the sixteenth century manages to combine a spear with a three-barrelled rifle. It's a collection that has all the appearance of a labour of love. There will be few other visitors when you go, and once you have discovered it, you will go again.

Running parallel to the rue des Archives at this point is the rue du Temple, which takes its name from the Knights Templar who once owned the whole of the Marais and a large part of Paris besides. The order had come into being after the First Crusade in order to protect pilgrims to the Holy Land, but in the way of these things the protection of pilgrims soon began to take second place to more rewarding activities. By the middle of the thirteenth century the Templars had acquired enormous wealth and the power that went with it. The entrance to their enclosure, surrounded by walls eight metres high, was at the top of the street, roughly opposite the rue des Fontaines-du-Temple. Within it they were a law unto themselves – and a threat to both Church and State. In 1307 the king of France and the pope made common cause to destroy them. It was the usual unsavoury partnership, messy but effective. The Templars were arrested, the more notable ones tortured and burned at the stake; by 1314 it was all over, and the king had the satisfaction of watching the Grand Master of the Order go up in flames on what is now the tip of the Île de la Cité. During the Revolution the tower which was inside the enclosure became a prison, where Louis XVI was held in the days before his execution. It was also suspected that his son, the young Louis XVII, was murdered here, so in 1808 the tower was demolished to prevent it from becoming a focus for Royalist sympathies.

We are at the wrong end of the rue du Temple for number 41, but if you find yourself in the area at another time, you should look inside the gateway of this quaint building. It is the only remaining example in Paris of an old coaching inn. The entrance leads into a cobbled yard, looked down on by a ring of slightly dilapidated windows. As you stand listening to the piano music which floats out from the dance studio that occupies part of the courtyard today, it is not difficult to imagine the scene when coaches festooned with luggage were clattering through to unload harassed English travellers arriving from Boulogne.

The rue du Temple itself is sprinkled with seventeenth-century buildings, and two of the neighbouring streets dispute the claim to have the oldest house in Paris. You can take your pick between 3, rue Volta and 51, rue de Montmorency. Both of them look suitably ancient, the one a half-timbered building with heavy wooden lintel in the Chinese quarter of the rue Volta, the other the home of Nicolas Flamel, its ground floor now a restaurant.

From here, there is an interesting detour to be made to the CONSERVATOIRE DES ARTS ET DES MÉTIERS near the top of the rue Saint-Martin. Interesting partly because of the site, which is the old priory of Saint-Martin-des-Champs, partly because it houses an enjoyable museum of technology. The automatic toys, among them a clockwork elephant and a dulcimer-player made for Marie-Antoinette, are a particular source of pride to the curator. You can see them all in operation on the first Wednesday of every month at 2.30 p.m. In other parts of the museum you will find items as diverse as Foucault's pendulum (with which he

OPPOSITE *The chapel of Saint-Martin-des-Champs, now part of the Conservatoire des Arts et Metiers.*

A languid funerary monument in the cemetery of Père Lachaise.

demonstrated in 1851 the movement of the earth), a grotesque nineteenth-century glass sculpture, an exhibit on the making of the Statue of Liberty, a 1932 Hispano Suiza, and the plane in which Blériot crossed the English Channel on 25 July 1909. It took him 26 minutes 30 seconds, and to appreciate the achievement you really need to have seen the aeroplane, which looks like an elongated tricycle with canvas flaps. That it ever got off the ground at all is surprising enough. Notice the unusual setting of this part of the museum, which is the former chapel of the priory. The other survivor of the old priory buildings is the thirteenth-century refectory, designed by the architect of the Sainte-Chapelle. This is at the moment undergoing restoration.

The place de la République has plenty of cheap clothes shops in the vicinity, but in other respects it is a less than inspiring place to end our walk. Huge and rather soulless, with a lumpish statue in the middle, it represents Haussmann at his worst. In fact, the whole neighbourhood is somewhat bleak; but though République may not itself do much to lift the spirits, you are at least well placed, at the intersection of several different Métro lines, to head for somewhere else. The main tourist destination to the east is the cemetery of PÈRE LACHAISE, named after Louis XIV's confessor but only turned into a cemetery at the time of the Revolution. Keen cemetery-goers will find here an impressive roll-call of the famous and the notorious. A plan of the graves can be bought for a few francs at the flower-shop next to the Métro entrance. This may prevent you from getting lost or may just increase your frustration when you do. The rows of stone monuments are not beautiful; even in summer there are fewer flowers than one might expect. So where should you go? The grave of Colette usually has a knot of flowers, as does that of Edith Piaf. Apart from them, my selection would probably take in the massive shrine of Héloise and Abélard, Rossini's cenotaph, the bust of the poet Alfred de Musset, with his request carved underneath that a willow be planted over his grave, the admirably restrained memorial of the Proust family, and perhaps also the well-tended graves of Amedeo Modigliani and Jeanne Hébuterne. On the latter the inscription reads '*Compagna Devota Fino All'Estremo Sacrifizio*', a melancholy recognition of the love that led her to throw herself from a fifth-floor window of her parents' house on the day after Modigliani's death. M. and Mme Hébuterne, unable to forgive their daughter's scandalous liaison with the painter, refused the request of friends for the couple to share a common grave. Jeanne's body was hustled off to a distant cemetery with the minimum of attention. Ten years were to pass before the two were reunited once again here in Père Lachaise.

More visited than most is Epstein's ugly, and now mutilated, monument to Oscar Wilde. The naked male angel caused something of a furore when it was first displayed. Later the offending member was lopped off, apparently by the head guardian – though whether as a keepsake or a blow for morality, or possibly to make a theological point, is uncertain. I suppose it could have been just a protest against a frightful work of art. A sad little biography on the back of the tomb seems largely devoted to Wilde's adolescent successes at Oxford – a first in

Mods., a first in Greats, the Newdigate prize – as though these trivial distinctions were all that could respectably be acknowledged about his life.

At the south-east corner of the cemetery, near the memorials to the victims of the concentration camps, is the *Mur des Fédérés*. A large plaque says simply '*Aux Morts de la Commune*'. It was here among the graves that the Paris Commune made its last stand on 27–28 May, 1871, and it was against the *Mur des Fédérés* that the survivors, all 147 of them, were shot. This was the end of two months of idealism and bloodshed which had begun with the refusal of the Communards, made up of revolutionaries and republicans among the working class, to accept the government's decision to surrender Paris to the Prussians. Having created the Commune, they tried to establish it by blood and fire, and were suppressed with equal barbarism. The place is now one of the prettiest parts of the cemetery.

Few visitors bother to wander beyond the confines of the cemetery into the streets of the 20th arrondissement. This is a pity. Unfrequented as they are, they have an atmosphere strikingly different from the areas of the city to which tourists are accustomed. In the leafy streets around the place Gambetta, the easier pace of life suggests a different kind of Paris.

The place de la Nation stands as the third point in a triangle made up by the place de la Bastille and the place de la République. It is a dull sort of square, which the central statue by Dalou, unpromisingly called *Triumph of the Republic*, does little to cheer. During the Revolution even more executions were carried out in this square than in the place de la Concorde, and somehow it never quite seems to have recovered. The flowers round Dalou's statue tend to look funereal rather than festive, and the whole square wears a slightly subdued look – open, anonymous, a bit lonely. In all, it is not the place for the end of the day. Best, perhaps, to go early one morning and then speed on by the RER to the woods and gardens of the Château de Vincennes.

7
The North and Montmartre

....

Paris seems reluctant to move too far from the Seine. Over the past 200 years it has spread itself grudgingly across the surrounding countryside, but it is still unusually compact for a major capital city. Until the late eighteenth century it was bounded to the north by what is now the line of the *grands boulevards*. Then, in the years leading up to the Revolution, the Farmers General Wall, with its 57 toll-houses, was constructed around the city, following the line of what have since become the outer boulevards. Even so, it was not until well into the nineteenth century that the newly included areas underwent much development. One of the most famous of these new districts sprang up around the recently built church of NOTRE-DAME-DE-LORETTE.

The church itself, a heavily classical affair facing the rue Lafitte, was a product of the 1820s and 1830s. Its dignity must have been sorely tried as the neighbouring streets fast became colonized by the dubious inhabitants who gave the quarter its reputation. When the rue Notre-Dame-de-Lorette was completed in 1834, a couple of years before the church, the developers were anxious to create the immediate impression of a thriving area. Accordingly, they installed tenants at low rents, even before the plaster was dry, on the one condition that they should hang curtains in the window to give the street the required appearance of being lived in. It was not everyone who was prepared to put up with damp walls in an unfashionable district, and most of the tenants were young girls in their teens or early twenties who had little to live on but their looks and their good humour. These were the *lorettes*. In the natural way of things they gravitated towards the sort of young men with modest incomes and artistic aspirations who had also been drawn to an area of low rents, so that by the mid-century Notre-Dame-de-Lorette had become synonymous with everything immoral that goes on when artists and girls of slender means are left to their own devices. As one writer remarked at the time, you had only to mention in the provinces that you had been to see a friend in Notre-Dame-de-Lorette to be branded as unknowable:

OPPOSITE *A traditional view of Montmartre. The steps of the rue Foyatier lead down from the Butte.*

159

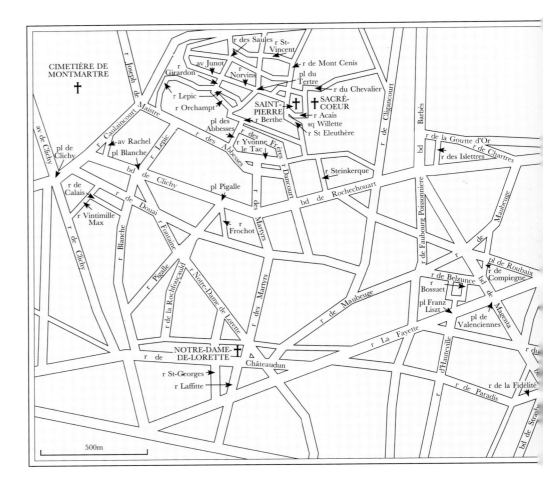

The prefect closes his door to you, the mayor no longer greets you, the priest will never accept you as his partner at cards, the justice of the peace forbids his son to hunt with you.

Time brings in its revenges, and today, although the shops and bars along the rue Notre-Dame-de-Lorette are far from fashionable, the net curtains in the windows above them proclaim the most solid respectability. The *lorettes*, however, are not quite forgotten. If you walk up to the place Saint-Georges, you can find a charming tribute to them below the bust of the caricaturist Gavarni in the centre of the square. Just beyond the monument is another small square, whose 100-year-old beech tree offers welcome shade in summer. It is typical of the restful little corners to be found all over Paris, for the most part unnoticed by visitors but much appreciated by the local residents.

The 9th arrondissement is not, on the whole, an enticing area to walk through, but for those who like to retrace the steps of the great, there is scarcely a street that cannot claim association with painters, writers and musicians of the nineteenth century. Delacroix lived in the rue Notre-Dame-de-Lorette, Géricault in the rue des Martyrs, Dumas, Zola and Ford Madox Brown in the rue Ballu, Apollinaire in the rue la Fontaine, Berlioz in the rue de Calais, Bizet and

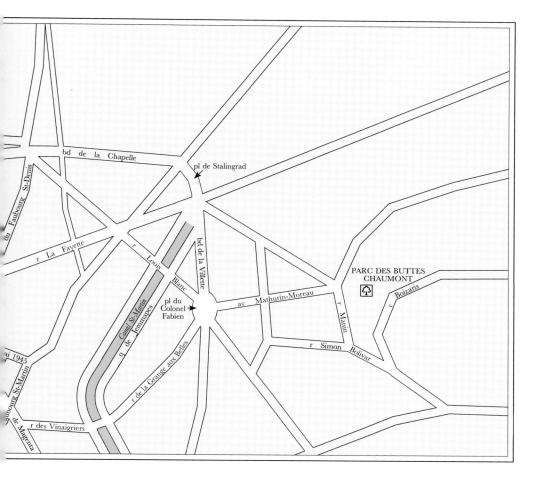

Hugo in the rue de la Tour-d'Auvergne, Chopin in the square d'Orléans, the
Goncourt brothers in the rue Saint-Georges – the list could be continued for a
page. If you walk along the rue de Douai, you will pass the house at number 50
where Turgenev lived with the opera singer Pauline Viardot and her husband. It
was here that Dickens came in 1856 for his somewhat unsuccessful meeting with
George Sand. ('Just the kind of woman in appearance whom you might suppose
to be the Queen's monthly nurse. Chubby, matronly, swarthy, black-eyed.') A
few yards away at 4, rue de Calais is the house where Berlioz died. Arnold Bennett lived here in the early years of the century, while he was working on *The Old
Wives' Tale*:

> Every afternoon and sometimes in the evening a distant violin used to play, very
> badly, six bars – no more – of an air of Verdi's over and over again; never any
> other tune! The sound was too faint to annoy me, but it was the most melan-
> choly thing that I have ever heard.

Most of those who once lived in these streets have left no more trace than the
notes of the violin recalled by Bennett, but there is one notable exception. At
14, rue de la Rochefoucauld the painter Gustave Moreau deliberately arranged
the top two floors of the building as a museum for his works. Though he

lived here until his death in 1898, it was in fact his parents' house, and there is another museum on the first floor, closed to the public, which he created out of his own personal and family memories. For most people the top two floors will be enough. There are something over 6000 of the artist's works exposed here, ranging from racks of drawings to huge canvases. Every available bit of wall space is crammed with paintings, creating an effect reminiscent of the crowded galleries of the eighteenth century. The form of the museum is a huge hall on the second floor with an attractive spiral staircase at one end, leading up to another large room, divided into two, where more of the paintings are displayed. Since most of the works are only identified by number, you are likely to need either a catalogue or a guided tour to take you through the jewelled figures and the heads dripping with blood. Moreau's work is not to everyone's taste, but there is an undeniable power in his distinctive mixture of the opulent and the perverse.

The 10th arrondissement, to the east, is even less likely to attract the casual visitor than the 9th, but it would be a pity not to take at least one stroll beside the Canal Saint-Martin. The neglected charm of the area has been eroded by some ugly buildings and the ever-increasing volume of traffic, but you can still sit in the little canal-side gardens above the creaking mechanism of the locks and try to shut out the noise of cars. It is curious to reflect, as you walk beside this placid waterway, that this was once the most fearful region in the neighbourhood of Paris. As recently as the eighteenth and early nineteenth centuries the whole district to the east of where we are walking was a mixture of open sewer and dumping ground for the carcasses of animals slaughtered in the nearby butchers' yards. In the place du Colonel-Fabien, then called the place du Combat, dogs and wild animals were pitted against each other in grisly fights. (The *place* still has something of the shape of an arena. Its wide central area, ringed by trees, is occupied by just one rather unusual street-lamp.) The cruelty, blood and stench of the eighteenth century were only a faint echo of the scenes that had marked this desolate landscape three hundred years earlier, when rotting bodies, up to 60 of them at a time, swung in chains from the great gibbet of Montfaucon. It was situated in the area now bounded by the Canal Saint-Martin and the rue de la Grange-aux-Belles, a massive structure formed by towering pillars of unhewn stone, 10 metres high, placed on a huge mound. There the executed men – and sometimes women – would hang until the sun, rain, crows and flies had done their work. 'The fayrest Gallowes that ever I saw', as the English traveller Thomas Coryate put it in the early seventeenth century.

From the place du Colonel-Fabien, now three-parts ringed with new buildings, the avenue Mathurin-Moreau leads up towards a much more cheering prospect. Practically no one who does not live in Paris visits the PARC DES BUTTES CHAUMONT, but it is an agreeable place, one of Haussmann's success stories. If you enter beside the Métro station, you will find a quiet pathway sloping round the wooded hills where sunbathers can improve their tan and parents can let their children off the leash. It is less well tended than some of the city's other gardens, but this section of it gives the impression of a genuine neighbourhood park which

OPPOSITE *Picturesque landscaping in the Parc des Buttes Chaumont, looking towards Montmartre.*

is used by the community. Don't leave, however, without walking up to the northern part of the Buttes Chaumont, for it is here that you will see the park at its most spectacular. Cunningly landscaped out of old quarries, it offers an imaginative arrangement of lake, grotto, bridges and waterfall that makes it one of the most picturesque spots in Paris.

As we head back towards Montmartre, we shall pass the imposing Gare de l'Est, and this might be the moment to take a Métro out to the CITÉ DES SCIENCES ET DE L'INDUSTRIE, which has been established at the north-east corner of Paris since 1986. Set in the urban wasteland around the Porte de la Villette, it is a hitech, open-plan museum where the escalators move among pipes, girders and miles of glass, and the furniture all looks suitably space-aged. The exhibitions inside change periodically, but there are always plenty of gadgets to play with and a plethora of instructive videos on everything from photosynthesis to high-speed trains, nuclear fission to the life of microbes. The emphasis everywhere is on audio-visual displays and visitor participation. To understand some of the instructions, it helps if you speak a little French, though many of the experiments are simple enough to be managed by guesswork. Twirl a black and white disc to produce colours, for example, or look at a red parrot for a while and then transfer your gaze to an empty cage, whereupon a green parrot materializes. More complicated is the stellarium, where a computer screen will teach you the constellations – as long as you press the right buttons. Other permanent attractions include a section on robots and a sort of greenhouse tunnel which demonstrates how tomatoes, melons and the like can be persuaded to grow without the benefit of soil. It is not necessarily a disadvantage to be completely unscientific; the less you know, the more impressive it all seems.

About the much vaunted *géode* I have mixed feelings. This giant silver dome, set in a pool of water that looks too small for it, is in fact a remarkable cinema. Its hemispherical screen covers 1000 square metres, so that the enveloping images seem almost to absorb the viewer into their intangible world. It ought to be extraordinarily exciting, but at least during my visit the films on show were tedious enough to neutralize even the most daring technology. It is an oddly contradictory experience to sit in what is billed as the world's most advanced cinema and watch films that look as though they were cobbled together in the 1950s from the left-overs of *Look at Life*.

Back at the Gare de l'Est there is little to detain us in the immediate vicinity, except the rue de Paradis, which is lined with shops selling porcelain and glass. The Limoges, in particular, is a temptation to extravagance. At 33bis we can make our way through the nineteenth-century entrance to Baccarat. This modern temple of glass has its museum-cum-salesroom on the first floor. It is perhaps more salesroom than museum, but worth a visit for the lavish displays of crystal. Much of the finest work is not for sale, including pieces made for various Paris Exhibitions. It is the *fin-de-siècle* era that produces some of the shapeliest designs.

As we make our way up towards the shabby curve of the outer boulevards, we shall pass the Gare du Nord, where for well over a hundred years travel-weary

OPPOSITE *The giant dome of the Géode in the Cité des Sciences et de l'Industrie.*

Britons have been emerging from the night train, stretching cramped limbs and venturing with quickened pulse into the streets of the city. It is by no means an exciting prospect that confronts one from the station entrance, but I feel a peculiar affection for it. For me, as for many others, it has been time and again the first view of Paris, and whether the absence has been short or long, the effect is magical. Ignore the large McDonald's to the right and focus on the red awnings of the Brasserie de Paris across the road, where the waiters wear black waistcoats and the tables march out into the street and the cars drive past with blaring horns. The Hotel Terminus Nord, with its balconies and shutters and familiar grey stone, dominates the scene. There are *pâtisseries* within sight and the same old newspaper kiosks. Across the road the Métro entrance still displays the elegant curves of the 1890s. We are back in Paris.

My way has always been to the south. An area I never used to visit, except in literature, was the huddle of streets centred on the rue de la Goutte-d'Or, just across the boulevard. This was the focus of Zola's great novel about the Paris of the Second Empire, *L'Assommoir*. What was in Zola's time a grim working-class area, where alcohol offered the only relief from lives of deadening poverty, now has the hectic bubbling atmosphere of a place where everything is bought and sold on the streets in shouted transactions that make the district a riot of colour and sound. Still unmistakably working-class, it has acquired a sort of fierce commercial vitality. The pervasive influence is North African. The rue de la Goutte-d'Or itself specializes in African fabrics, displaying bolts of exotic cloth in every other doorway. Just to the south, around the Barbès Métro stop, the area has become an unofficial bazaar. Salesmen under the arches sell suitcases, watches, sewing machines, whatever happens to have come their way during the week. Shifty-looking characters hand out cards for gurus who offer defence against evil spirits – 'even your most desperate problems will be solved'. Along the pavements of the boulevard, between the street-stalls, Arabs hold out an assortment of rings, bracelets, watches, cameras, accosting you in a furtive whisper as you pass – '*c'est bon, c'est pas cher*'. The atmosphere has an exhilarating breath of remote places and alien cultures.

In the nineteenth century this quarter was just beside the hated Farmers General Wall, where taxes were levied on all manner of goods being brought into the capital. Thackeray, the author of *Vanity Fair*, was stopped here on his way into Paris in the 1830s and watched while the green-clad customs men probed the straw of the peasants' carts with their long needles. To bring a cow into the city cost 24 francs at the time, a hog nine francs, a hundredweight of tallow candles three francs. Small wonder that Parisians murmured against the wall.

The local toll-gate for this area, the Barrière Poissonnière, was just about where the Métro station of Barbès-Rochechouart stands today, and since neither our time nor our movements are restricted, we might take this opportunity to board the Métro – a novel experience here, since it runs above ground – and follow the direct line out to the Porte de Clignancourt. The goal of this excursion is the Flea Market that sprawls across the neighbouring streets. When you emerge from the Métro stop, head past the discouraging rows of parked tour buses and along the avenue Porte de Clignancourt. The real market (actually several different markets run together) only begins when you get beyond the boulevard Périphérique and enter a village of stalls pervaded by the smell of incense. Furniture, clothes, cutlery, jewellery, records, musical instruments, ethnic bric-à-brac of every description – whatever you want, you will find it on sale in some form or other. The only problem then is to get it home.

Back at the Métro station of Barbès-Rochechouart, the outer boulevards stretch east and west along the line of the old tax wall. During the *belle époque*, cabs rattled along these wide streets, bringing fashionable Parisians out to sample the more or less daring pleasures of the boulevard. Now tour-buses do much the same for nightly flocks of Americans, Japanese, Germans, Italians and Britons. But the entertainments on offer have changed. The area first became popular in the middle of the nineteenth century when crowds would gather for the sort of dances pictured by Renoir in his *Bal au Moulin de la Galette*. The Elysée-Montmartre, at 72, boulevard Rochechouart, was one of the first of the sumptuous dance halls that became a feature of the boulevard. It has survived here on the corner of the rue de Steinkerque from the beginning of one century to the end of the next. Today the ground floor is spoiled by an ugly entrance that looks as though it ought to lead into a bingo hall, but above the doorway are the remains of happier days: surrounded by an arch of flowers, the image of a dancing girl invites us in to join the company.

Later, the fashion for cabaret was started a few doors away when Rodolphe Salis opened his Chat Noir at number 84 in 1881. This was afterwards taken over by Aristide Bruant, who strode amongst his audience in the red scarf and broad-brimmed felt hat depicted by Lautrec, insulting them, abusing them, swearing at them and generally making them feel they had had their money's worth. Edmond de Goncourt watched his performance with dismay:

> To think that those society women, without the protection of a fan, without even a blush on their cheeks, listening to the man from close to, smiled and clapped their pretty aristocratic hands at words no different from the obscene scribblings on walls from which they avert their eyes.

On 5 October, 1889 Charles Zidler initiated a new craze when he opened the Moulin Rouge a short way along the boulevard, on the corner of the place Blanche. The atmosphere of this world was caught for ever by the crippled figure of Henri de Toulouse-Lautrec, whose studio was nearby, first in the rue Tourlaque and later in the avenue Frochot. He painted the can-can dancers, like Jane Avril and La Goulue, and the haunts of pleasure where they worked, conveying both the feverish gaiety of the period and also the inevitable undertow of melancholy. The fate of La Goulue cannot have been unusual. After her moment of glory, when money was showered upon her and princes were at her feet, she ended up as a rag-picker along the boulevards.

Henri de Toulouse-Lautrec,
Jane Avril dancing, c. *1892.*

And yet it is hard to persuade oneself that things were not better in the past. There is something inescapably depressing about the modern Moulin Rouge with its commissionaires, its sequined dresses and its hints of naughtiness, all carefully tailored to a respectable audience. In a way I prefer the desolate stretch of neon sleaze that runs from the place Blanche to the place de Clichy. Sleazy is what it is, of course, and yet somehow a festive note keeps breaking through. It's hard to see anything very sinister in a shop selling discount chain-link underwear and leather hoods, when a busload of elderly Japanese couples clearly find it so amusing. One place offers Paris T-shirts and models of the Eiffel Tower, another promises feats of athletic copulation, between them a perfectly modest restaurant sets out its tables. Everything is grist to the tourist mill. The district's aspirations to depravity are continually undercut by the blandness of its clientèle. The polyglot masses browse along the northern side of the boulevard with much the same cheerful, half-awakened interest that they give to the Grande Galerie in the Louvre. And in much the same way they have themselves photographed in front of the exhibits. It's a lively, diverting scene, but for the potential buyer the warning is *caveat emptor*. Sex, along with other luxury goods, is now taxed at 33% by the French Government, which can make the sight of tired bodies an expensive treat.

Today the place Pigalle is looking even tattier than the rest of the area, but its name still has a certain resonance borrowed from the status it enjoyed 100 years ago. At number 9, where now the Narcisse offers white flesh and black leather, stood the Café de la Nouvelle Athènes. George Moore was once a habitué:

> I did not go to Oxford or Cambridge, but I went to the 'Nouvelle Athènes'. I can hear the glass door of the café grate on the sand as I open it. I can recall the smell of every hour. In the morning that of eggs frizzling in butter, the pungent cigarette, coffee and bad cognac; at five o'clock the fragrant odour of absinthe; and soon after the steaming soup ascends from the kitchen; and as the evening advances, the mingled smells of cigarettes, coffee, and weak beer.

The reference to absinthe is apposite. It was here that Degas painted his two forlorn drinkers slumped in front of glasses of the opalescent liquid that was the district's trademark. Elsewhere the 'absinthe hour' ran through the early evening, in Pigalle it never ended.

Directly across the road from the Nouvelle Athènes was another famous café, favoured by Manet, the Rat Mort. When the beer pump failed to work at the opening party, it was found to be blocked by a dead rat. Quite unabashed, the proprietor promptly renamed his café and had scenes from the life and death of the rat painted on the walls and ceiling. This sort of trench humour seems to be an integral part of the Montmartre milieu. It was the world of the *apache*, where Edith Piaf acquired the name of the sparrow of Pigalle and figures like Maurice Chevalier and later Yves Montand made their way to stardom from the old music-halls of the boulevard.

Beyond the Moulin Rouge the place de Clichy marks the point where the seedy life of the boulevards gives way to the innocent but unexciting *quartier de*

l'Europe. For a piquant contrast to the world of Pigalle, you might board the Métro again at Clichy and make the short trip to SAINT-DENIS a few kilometres to the north. The cathedral was built in the twelfth and thirteenth centuries on the presumed site of the saint's grave and is of particular interest for the tombs it contains of the kings and queens of France. The contents of the tombs were scattered during the Revolution, but the remarkable funerary monuments survived. It is fortunately no longer necessary to see them by guided tour, since visitors are supplied with headphones which cunningly pick up a signal from listening posts in front of the various tombs. This can have hazards of its own if one drifts into the orbit of other listeners, but on the whole it is a good deal less irritating than the average human guide. Among the most striking monuments are the thirteenth-century effigy of Isabella of Aragon and the fine Italian sculpture of Louis XII and Anne of Brittany, carved in the early sixteenth century. Germain Pilon's statues of Henri II and Catherine de' Medici date from later in the same century. (The original effigy of Catherine by Primaticcio had been altogether too deathlike for her taste, so Pilon was called in to provide a more soothing alternative.) Most moving of all is the superb monument to François I and Claude of France for which Philibert Delorme and Pierre Bontemps were primarily responsible. The pitiful delicacy of these two figures laid out in death is a triumph of sixteenth-

A detail from the twelfth-century west front of the cathedral of Saint-Denis, showing the saint's last communion.

century sculpture. It is sad that visitors can only get a partial view of them, although the copies in the Musée des Monuments Français give one an idea of their beauty (p. 77).

For tombs of a different sort we can return to the boulevard de Clichy, where a conveniently situated undertaker marks the corner of the avenue Rachel, which will take us up to the Cimetière de Montmartre. Its illustrious dead include, as one would expect, a high proportion of artists, writers and musicians, among them Gautier, Zola, Dumas *fils*, Murger, Degas, Offenbach, Berlioz and the Goncourts. Here also you will find the stone that originally marked the grave of Stendhal, now set into the more elaborate memorial provided by later admirers. It says simply *Arrigo Beyle, Milanese, Scrisse, Amo, Visse* and then gives the date of his death, 23 March, 1842.

Among the sloping graves of the cemetery, we have already started to climb what is called the Butte, the hill at the top of which is the real Montmartre. Until this century the district was little more than a rustic village. The origins of its name, which perhaps go back to a Roman temple (hence Mons Mercurii or Mons Martis), are a matter of dispute. My own preference, for quite unhistorical reasons, is the legend which derives it from the martyrdom of St Denis, who brought the gospel to the Paris region in the third century and was executed on the orders of the Roman prefect. Just off the place des Abbesses, at 11, rue Yvonne-le-Tac, is the chapel built in the nineteenth century to replace the one which marked the site of his execution. The Roman soldiers who were charged with the job decided, as many weary tourists have done since, that the hill was too steep for comfort. They accordingly beheaded the future saint when they were only half-way up. He then surprised them by picking up his head and taking it with him to the top of the hill, where he washed it at a spring (now the Fontaine Saint-Denis) before striding on with the head under his arm for another six kilometres. Two hundred years later St Geneviève erected the church of Saint-Denis at the place where he finally died.

The chapel we can see today in the rue Yvonne-le-Tac is an unlovely building, of interest only as the site of the original chapel. It was here, on 15 August, 1534, that Ignatius Loyola and his six companions, among them François Xavier, took the vows which marked the foundation of the Jesuit order. Inside the chapel is a copy of the plaque which was put up by the Jesuits in the early seventeenth century to commemorate this event.

One other reason for strolling, or, if the afternoon is hot, staggering to the place des Abbesses is to admire the entrance to its Métro station. This is one of the original art nouveau creations of Hector Guimard, who brought out the designs in 1899. Although known by its French name, art nouveau never had quite the success in France that it achieved elsewhere in Europe. By the beginning of the twentieth century its vogue was already on the wane and the new Métro stations received a frosty welcome from the public. 'Harmful to the honour of French taste' was one characteristically pompous judgement that greeted their appearance. In spite of this, the basic design continued to be used on the ten Métro lines

ABOVE *The tomb of Émile Zola, one of many writers and artists buried in the Cimetière de Montmartre.*

OPPOSITE *The bell-tower of Saint-Denis, one of the earliest of France's great gothic churches.*

until 1914 – which is why we can still see a number of them scattered about the city, instantly recognizable by their ornate railings and the beautiful wrought-iron tendrils that curve round the canopies of the entrance. Abbesses is an excellent example. (If you arrive here by Métro and are willing to forgo the lift, you can also see the recent murals by the Montmartre Artists' Collective which provide colourful decoration for the walls beside the spiral staircase.)

The Métro system itself has been in operation since 1900 and now has thirteen lines covering just under 200 kilometres. Especially at night, its long white-tiled corridors used to have an eerie, almost nightmarish quality that was woven into many a visitor's memories of the city. The old austerity has now given way to endless panels of advertisements. Other things remain the same. I have never yet seen a *mutilé de guerre* claim his right to one of the numbered seats, but stickers in the carriages still assert it. On the whole, clean platforms, clean trains and some increasingly handsome stations make travel as painless as possible, particularly now that the vexatious automatic doors which used to swing shut just as one reached the platform have fallen into disuse. The Paris Métro can still excite positive affection. Does any visitor to London look back on the experience of the underground with other than a shudder of distaste?

By the time you reach the place Émile-Goudeau, all but the fittest will be ready for another rest. Though unprovided with a café, the leafy square makes a pleasant stopping place. Sitting on one of the benches under the trees, you can glance across to the somewhat blank building at numbers 11bis–13, which is the reconstructed Bateau-Lavoir. The original wooden structure, dating from the 1880s, was known as the Trapper's Hut on account of its curious appearance. Rechristened the Bateau-Lavoir by Max Jacob and André Salmon, it became famous in the years before World War I as the birthplace of Cubism, where Picasso painted *Les Demoiselles d'Avignon*. Among other artists and writers who lived here were MacOrlan, Modigliani, Van Dongen and Juan Gris. A fire in 1970 destroyed the building, which was reconstructed eight years later.

The apotheosis of the Bateau-Lavoir was the so-called *banquet Rousseau*, organized by Picasso in 1908 in honour of le Douanier Rousseau. The guests included Gertrude and Leo Stein, Alice Toklas, Braque, Vlaminck, André Salmon and Marie Laurencin. By the time Apollinaire arrived with the guest of honour, most of the company were already drunk and Marie Laurencin had managed to fall down among the patisseries which had been stacked in the cloakroom for lack of space. (Apollinaire brusquely ejected her from the party.) Rousseau himself was some 30 years older than the rest of the guests and there has always been some question as to whether the whole affair was really an elaborate joke at his expense, but if such was the case, he was blissfully unaware of it. He took his seat at the centre of a raised platform and then, while the lantern above him dripped hot wax on his head, got steadily drunker as songs were sung and poems recited in his praise. After contributing a few airs on his violin, he fell asleep and was finally taken home by the Steins. In the meantime, the proprietor of the local cabaret had wandered in with his donkey and André Salmon had

A detail from Renoir's Bal au Moulin de la Galette, *1876*.

upset Gertrude Stein by chewing soap and then frothing at the mouth in a feigned attack of delirium tremens. It was an evening for the writers of memoirs, and fortunately there were plenty on hand to do it justice.

If you bear left out of the square along the cobbled rue d'Orchampt, you will come, within a few metres, to the windmill which stands at the junction of the rue Lepic and the rue Girardon. Now called the Radet and occupied by a restaurant, this mill is actually on the site of the old Moulin de la Galette which became famous as a dance hall in the nineteenth century. Its atmosphere is wonderfully evoked in the Renoir painting that hangs in the Musée d'Orsay (pp. 93–6). A few yards down the rue Lepic, opposite the rue Tholozé, is another windmill, often confused with it, which later took over the name of Moulin de la Galette. This is a much older structure in which the mill's owners, the Debray brothers, were supposed to have made their heroic stand against the advancing Russians in 1814. Three of them were killed in the fight, the fourth was then quartered by the heartless Russians and nailed in pieces to the sails of his own mill. It is a stirring tale, but historical evidence gives it little support.

A short way up the rue Girardon, the avenue Junot sweeps round to your left. It was here, at number 11, that Maurice Utrillo lived for a time after World War I. An amiable alcoholic, he was shut up in a room with barred windows by his mother Suzanne Valadon. One of his few distractions was to wait until he saw a policeman cycling up the hill past his window and then shout *Vive l'anarchie!* at the top of his voice.

In the other direction, the rue Norvins takes you past Jean Marais's statue of a bronze figure striding out of the wall – an eye-catching tribute to the writer Marcel Aymé, after whom this little square at the crossroads is named. Further up the rue Norvins, close to the place du Tertre, number 22bis was once the site of the country house known as la Folie Sandrin. For the first half of the nineteenth century this was a high-class mental asylum, directed for part of that time by the famous Dr Blanche who later moved his clinic to Passy. Jacques Hillairet lists a fascinating collection of patients, among them the writer Jacques Arago, who had composed a book 62 pages long without once using the letter 'a'. Gérard de Nerval also spent time here, as did one of Marie-Antoinette's ladies-in-waiting who had gone mad because she was unable to marry Robespierre.

It is true, of course, that tourism has taken hold of Montmartre to an extent that often leaves the area around Sacré-Coeur choked with big men in check trousers; massive tour buses now grind their way through the narrow streets, and toy-town convoys of linked carriages do their best to bring the setting one stage closer to Disneyland. But away from the centres of activity many of the streets of the Butte retain something of their former tranquillity. It is easy, still, to turn a corner and fancy oneself in the scene of a painting by Utrillo. Stroll, for example, past the end of the rue de l'Abreuvoir and enter the square Suzanne-Buisson. In this shaded enclosure you are walking through the grounds of the eighteenth-century folly known as the Château des Brouillards, where de Nerval lived for a while in 1846. (He thought at the time of buying one of the vineyards for which Montmartre was famous.) Today, it is a secluded spot where local children play and local men meet for *boules*. At the centre is a statue of St Denis, standing above the fountain where he washed his severed head, a venerable presence in a peaceful garden.

A short step from here, at the intersection of the rue des Saules and the rue Saint-Vincent is the cabaret of the Lapin Agile. Earlier known as the Cabaret des Assassins, it acquired its present name in 1880 when André Gill painted a sign for it depicting an agile rabbit, with one foot in a saucepan, balancing a bottle on his arm. A copy of this still decorates the façade. Much painted – and much patronized – by Utrillo, the Lapin Agile was in the early years of the century a meeting place for many of the artists and writers associated with the Bateau-Lavoir.

Unexpected stardom came to the donkey belonging to the owner, Frédé, when Roland Dorgelès sent in an abstract painting to the Salon des Indépendants which had in fact been painted by the donkey swishing its tail. On the 18 March, 1910 a lawyer, who imagined that he was being called out for a case of adultery, was brought to the Lapin Agile to notarize the donkey's efforts. The aim, Dorgelès said, was to expose the ridiculous nature of some of the works sent to the Salon. Later, the painting, poetically entitled *Et le soleil s'endormit sur l'Adriatique*, was sold for a creditable 500 francs.

Today the Lapin Agile continues to function as a cabaret, where those whose tastes do not run to the entertainments of the boulevard can sit in a decor still recognizable as that of the 1900s and listen to *chansonniers* who carry on the tradition of Aristide Bruant, himself once the owner of the Lapin.

The original sign painted by André Gill is now displayed in the nearby Musée de Montmartre at 12, rue Cortot. Dating from the mid seventeenth century, this is the oldest house in Montmartre and was lived in by Renoir in 1875. From its windows you can look out on the only vineyard left in Paris. The museum itself is slightly disappointing. More thought has been given to cashing in on the tourist trade than to illustrating the history of the house or explaining the artistic traditions of Montmartre. Even so, there are some interesting exhibits, including a copy of the painting by Frédé's donkey and two rooms devoted to Bruant and Modigliani.

The garden of the Musée de Montmartre runs down to the rue Saint-Vincent, close to the site of the house where Berlioz lived from 1834 to 1836 with Harriet Smithson, on the corner of the rue du Mont-Cenis. It was here that he wrote *Harold in Italy* and *Benvenuto Cellini*. Beside the new apartment block which now occupies this site, we can turn back and climb the steep flight of steps towards the place du Tertre. Just before reaching the square we cross the rue du Chevalier-de-la-Barre which curves round behind Sacré-Coeur. This was formerly the rue des Rosiers, where the two generals, Lecomte and Clément Thomas, were shot on 19 March, 1871 at the start of the Commune. The National Guard had previously collected 171 cannon from around the city and brought them up here to keep them from the victorious Prussians. When General Lecomte was sent to recover them, he was arrested. Along with Clément Thomas, who had been picked up on the boulevard de Clichy, he was executed in front of the wall which stood roughly opposite the present site of the bell-tower of Sacré-Coeur. After this there was no turning back until the Commune came to its bloody end two months later among the graves of Père Lachaise.

The ancient place du Tertre, packed with restaurant tables, swarming with tourists and overrun by artists, is the sort of place one cannot see without wishing one had got there 100 years earlier. To the modern visitor it offers the spectacle of tourism at its most crass. The paintings that are the square's stock-in-trade used to be variations on the theme of the tearful clown; more recently they have been supplemented by a fashion for imitation naïve. Presumably someone must buy them, but even the most unworldly tourist might be moved to cynicism by their

The cabaret of the Lapin Agile acquired its name from the sign painted for it by André Gill.

ABOVE *Gismondi's modern bronze doors for Saint-Pierre complement the stark simplicity of the ancient church.*

OPPOSITE *Completed in 1910, Sacré-Coeur shows little sign of age because of the nature of its marble, which becomes whiter with time.*

production-line uniformity. At number 6, on the edge of the square, you will find the celebrated Restaurant de la Mère Catherine, supposedly founded by the same Cossacks who dealt so harshly with the patriotic Debrays. Elsewhere, the cafés tend to be overpriced and overcrowded, the shops full of junk, the locals rapacious. Best to walk round beside the trees, which in one form or another have graced the square since the seventeenth century, and move on to the little church of SAINT-PIERRE just to the east.

Completed in the twelfth century, this appealing church is often neglected in favour of its monumental neighbour. For my part, I could cheerfully dispense with another visit to Sacré-Coeur, but Saint-Pierre has an atmosphere that will always draw me back. It is an unusual mixture. The modern stained glass and the fine bronze doors by Gismondi in the west façade are an imaginative addition to a church that can also boast columns that once belonged to a Roman temple. It is the sense of age that predominates. As one stands at the entrance and looks down towards the altar, the weight of the centuries seems to be splaying the arches of the building outward. To the north of the church is another door by Gismondi, depicting the Resurrection. If you look through the gaps, you can just see into the derelict little cemetery where the great explorer Bougainville lies buried.

The whole church is a moving contrast to the great white mass of SACRÉ-COEUR which now overshadows it. The basilica was designed in part as a gesture of expiation for France's humiliating defeat by the Prussians in 1870, but the construction took so long that it was not actually completed until 1910 and not consecrated until after World War I. Inside, the telephone guide will list for you the great men who have come to worship here; they include Max Jacob, Utrillo and Pope John Paul II. Of the building itself we are told that it is 'a grandiose ensemble', and that seems a fair enough summary of what must surely be Paris's most lifeless church. The particular stone used in its construction, which gets whiter as it gets older, gives the whole edifice a sepulchral pallor. My own impulse would be to leave it to the post-card designers and turn instead to the square Willette.

Here, with your elbows resting on the parapet, you can look out over one of the loveliest prospects that any city in the world has to offer. Laid out before you are Notre-Dame and Saint-Eustache, the Panthéon and the Pompidou Centre, the golden dome of the Invalides and, yes, like it or not, the Tour Montparnasse. Many places have a legend associated with them that if you ring the bell or touch the stone or throw a coin into the fountain, you will inevitably return. I feel the same about this view from Sacré-Coeur. Having looked out over the scene of so much history and so much beauty and so many memories of personal happiness, how can one not return?

Appendices

....

CHRONOLOGY OF EVENTS • RULERS
ARTISTS AND PATRONS • OPENING TIMES

CHRONOLOGY OF EVENTS

BC

*c.*350 — Celtic tribesmen settle at 'Louk-teih' (place of the marsh)

53 — 'Lutetia' first mentioned by the Romans in Caesar's 'Gallic Wars'

52 — The Gallic rebellion led by Vercingetorix. The city is occupied by the legate Titus Labienus

AD

*c.*280 — Martyrdom of St Denis, first bishop of Paris and patron saint of France

*c.*360 — City becomes known as Paris

451 — According to legend, the city is spared from the Huns through the intercession of St Geneviève, patron saint of Paris

498 — Baptism of Clovis I, making him the first Christian ruler of the area

508 — Clovis I establishes Paris as his capital

732 — Charles Martel defeats the Moors at Poitiers

751 — The Carolingian Dynasty takes power.

843 — Division of the Frankish Empire by the Treaty of Verdun and the start of modern France

885/7 — Siege of Paris, successfully defended by Count Eudes

987 — The Capetians assume power and Paris is established once more as the capital

1163 — Laying of the foundation stone of Notre-Dame

*c.*1200 — Work begins on the fortress of the Louvre. Philippe II grants charter to the University

1229 — Treaty of Paris brings an end to the Albigensian Wars

1257 — Robert de Sorbon establishes the college that will later become the Sorbonne

1302 — French Parliament moved to Paris

1307 — Suppression of the Order of Knights Templar

1337 — Outbreak of the Hundred Years War between England and France

1358 — Death of Etienne Marcel, Provost of the Paris merchants, after a failed revolt against the monarchy

1370 — Building work begins on the Bastille

1382 — Maillotin uprising crushed

1411 — Start of the civil war between the Armagnacs and the Burgundians. Paris supports the latter

1420 — Henry V of England enters Paris

1431 — Joan of Arc burned at the stake in Rouen

1436 — Control of Paris regained from the English

1453 — End of the Hundred Years War

1463 — François Villon exiled from Paris

1527 — François I re-establishes the royal court in Paris

1563 — Catherine de' Medici commissions the Tuileries

1572 — Massacre of St Bartholomew's Day

1588 — Henri III is driven out of Paris during the Revolt of the Barricades

1598 — Henri IV issues the Edict of Nantes

1610 — Henri IV is assassinated in Paris by Ravaillac

1615 — The Palais du Luxembourg is built for Marie de' Medici

1635 — Foundation of the Académie Française

1648–53 — The Fronde

1673 — Death of Molière

1685	Revocation of the Edict of Nantes	**1848**	Louis-Philippe abdicates following the February Revolution	**1900**	Opening of the Métro service. Oscar Wilde dies in the Hôtel d'Alsace
1715	End of Louis XIV's long reign				
1756	Soufflot begins work on the Panthéon	**1852**	Foundation of the Second Empire	**1919**	The League of Nations is established at the Paris peace conference
1778	Voltaire's triumphant return to Paris	**1853–69**	Baron Haussmann's radical building plan transforms Paris		
1789	The storming of the Bastille, marking the start of the French Revolution	**1855**	The first of a series of International Exhibitions opens in Paris	**1924**	Seventh Summer Olympics held in Paris. André Breton publishes his Surrealist Manifesto
1791	Louis XVI and Marie-Antoinette are arrested while attempting to flee the country	**1863**	Salon des Refusés	**1940**	German troops occupy Paris
		1867	The city stages its second International Exhibition	**1944**	The Liberation of Paris by allied forces
1792	France declared a republic	**1870/1**	France is defeated in the Franco-Prussian war.	**1958**	Establishment of the Fifth Republic with Charles de Gaulle as president
1793	Execution of Louis XVI. Assassination of Marat				
		1871	The Communard insurrection is violently suppressed		
1794	Danton and Robespierre are guillotined			**1962**	André Malraux, Minister of Culture, drafts a law to protect the city's ancient monuments
		1874	First Impressionist exhibition		
1804	Napoleon crowned emperor at Notre-Dame	**1880**	Bastille Day is declared a national holiday		
1814	Allied troops occupy Paris. Restoration of the monarchy	**1883**	The Orient Express starts to operate from Paris	**1968**	Demonstrations by students and workers bring the nation to a standstill
1815	Napoleon's attempt to regain power ends at the Battle of Waterloo	**1884**	First showing at the Salon des Indépendants	**1977**	Opening of the Pompidou Centre. Jacques Chirac is installed as the first elected Mayor of Paris
		1889	The Eiffel Tower is completed		
1830	Charles X is overthrown in the July Revolution	**1894–1906**	The Dreyfus Affair divides opinion in France		
1837	Opening of the first railway line in France between Paris and Saint-Germain en Laye	**1895**	The Lumière brothers organise the first performance of a film in Paris	**1989**	Opening of the Louvre Pyramid to coincide with the Bicentenary celebrations

RULERS

Merovingian Dynasty

Childeric I	c.457–481
Clovis I	481–511
Childebert I King of Paris	511–558
Clotaire I King of Soissons	511–558
Clotaire I sole king	558–561
Charibert I King of Paris	561–567
Chilperic I King of Soissons	561–584
Clotaire II King of Soissons	584–629
Clotaire II sole king	613–623
Dagobert I	623–639
Clovis II King of Neustria & Burgundy	639–656
Dagobert II King of Austrasia	656–661
Childeric II King of Austrasia	661–670
Childeric II sole king	670–673
Thierry III King of Neustria	673–679
Thierry III sole king	679–690
Clovis III	690–694
Childebert III	694–711
Dagobert III	711–715
Chilperic II	715–720
Thierry IV King of Neustria & Burgundy	720–737
Interregnum	737–742
Childeric III	742–751

Carolingian Dynasty

Pepin the Short	751–768
Charlemagne	768–814
Louis I (the Pious)	814–840
Charles I (the Bald)	840–877
Louis II (the Stammerer)	877–879
Louis III & Carloman	879–882
Carloman	882–884
Charles II (the Fat)	884–887
Count Eudes	887–898
Charles III (the Simple)	898–922
Louis IV (d'Outremer)	936–954
Lothaire	954–986
Louis V	986–987

Capetian Dynasty

Hugh Capet	987–996
Robert (the Pious)	996–1031
Henri I	1031–1060
Philippe I	1060–1108
Louis VI (the Fat)	1108–1137
Louis VII (the Young)	1137–1180
Philippe II (Augustus)	1180–1223
Louis VIII (the Lion)	1223–1226
Louis IX (St Louis)	1226–1270
Philippe III (the Bold)	1270–1285
Philippe IV (the Fair)	1285–1314
Louis X (the Headstrong)	1314–1316
Jean I	1316
Philippe V (the Long)	1316–1322
Charles IV (the Fair)	1322–1328

House of Valois

Philippe VI	1328–1350
Jean II (the Good)	1350–1364
Charles V (the Wise)	1364–1380
Charles VI (the Well-Beloved)	1380–1422
Charles VII (the Victorious)	1422–1461
Louis XI	1461–1483
Charles VIII	1483–1498
Louis XII	1498–1515
François I	1515–1547
Henri II	1547–1559
François II	1559–1560
Charles IX	1560–1574
Henri III	1574–1589

House of Bourbon

Henri IV	1589–1610
Louis XIII	1610–1643
Louis XIV (the Sun King)	1643–1715
Louis XV	1715–1774
Louis XVI	1774–1793

First Republic	1792–1804

First Empire

Napoleon Bonaparte	1804–1814

House of Bourbon

Louis XVIII	1814–1824
Charles X	1824–1830

House of Orléans

Louis-Philippe	1830–1848

Second Republic	1848–1851

Second Empire

Napoleon III	1852–1870

ARTISTS AND PATRONS

Baltard, Victor (1805–74) architect: built Les Halles (demolished 1971. One pavilion rebuilt at Nogent-sur-Marne): his church of Saint-Augustin has an unusual iron construction.

Bartholdi, Frédéric Auguste (1834–1904) sculptor: reduced version of his 'Statue of Liberty' on the pont de Grenelle.

Bonnard, Pierre (1867–1947) painter, illustrator and designer: influenced by the Impressionists and associated with Gauguin. Best known for his delicately lit interiors and nude studies.

Bontemps, Pierre (c.1505/10–68) leading tomb sculptor of the period: reclining effigies in Saint-Denis.

Boucher, François (1703–70) rococo painter and designer: his lighthearted, often erotic approach epitomized French taste in the pre-Revolutionary period. Mme de Pompadour's favourite artist.

Boulanger, Louis (1806–67) romantic painter, a follower of Delacroix.

Boullier, Jean (c.1630–1714) baroque architect, a disciple of Le Vau. Hôtel Salé.

Brancusi, Constantin (1876–1957) Romanian sculptor, active mainly in Paris. Worked with Modigliani, Studio reconstructed in Pompidou Centre.

Braque, Georges (1882–1963) Painter, linked initially with the Fauves but best known as the co-founder of Cubism with Picasso.

Brosse, Salomon de (c.1562–1626) architect: Related to the Du Cerceau family. Designed the Palais du Luxembourg.

Bruant, Libéral (c.1635–97) architect: unusual design of Salpêtrière chapel (c.1670). Hôtel des Invalides (1670–7).

Chagall, Marc (1887–1985) Russian painter and stained glass designer: member of the School of Paris. Although mainly active in France, Chagall's lyrical paintings remained firmly rooted in his Jewish and Russian background.

Champaigne, Philippe de (1602–74) Flemish portrait painter who settled in Paris in 1621: his principal patrons were Marie de' Medici and Cardinal Richelieu.

Claude Gellée ('Le Lorrain') (1600–82) painter and draughtsman, the supreme exponent of classical landscape painting.

Clouet family of portrait painters, the most significant of whom were Jean (d.1540/1) and his son François (c.1510–72).

Corot, Jean-Baptiste-Camille (1796–1875) versatile landscape painter. His lyrical, Italianate pictures won him great praise at the Salon, but his earlier, naturalistic style was more influential on later artists.

Courbet, Gustave (1819–77) painter and founder of the Realist movement. Courbet painted landscapes, portraits and scenes of modern life, but much of his work had a political content and he was imprisoned for his part in the destruction of the Vendôme Column.

Coysevox, Antoine (1640–1720) baroque sculptor: noted for lively portrait busts. Statues and reliefs at Versailles.

Dalou, Aimé-Jules (1838–1902) sculptor: fled to England in 1871 after taking part in the Commune. *Triumph of the Republic* (place de la Nation). *Memorial to Delacroix* (Jardin de Luxembourg).

Daumier, Honoré (1808–79) caricaturist, painter and sculptor: best known for his savage political cartoons, directed against Louis-Philippe and his ministers. His paintings, by contrast, contained sympathetic portrayals of the poorer elements in Parisian society.

Davioud, Gabriel Jean Antoine (1823–81) architect, worked with Haussmann: Notable fountains at place Saint-Michel and place de l'Observatoire.

Degas, Hilaire Germain Edgar (1834–1917) painter, draughtsman and sculptor: exhibited at all but one of the Impressionist shows. Celebrated for his depictions of horse-racing and ballet scenes.

Delacroix, Eugène (1798–1863) leading painter of the Romantic movement, characterised by his dashing use of colour: depicted many arab scenes following his travels in north Africa. Notable murals in Chapelle des Anges, Saint-Sulpice.

Delaunay, Robert (1885–1941) painter: developed an individual form of Cubism which influenced the Futurists.

Delorme, Philibert (c.1515–70) architect to Henri II and Diane de Poitiers: much of his work has been destroyed, but the tomb of François I (Saint-Denis) survives and part of the exquisite rood screen at Saint-Étienne du Mont is attributed to him.

Derain, André (1880–1954) leading Fauvist painter: also influenced by Cézanne and primitive African art. Like Braque, he produced designs for the 'Ballet Russe'.

Desjardins, Martin (1637–94) Flemish sculptor, resident in Paris from c.1670. Statues at Versailles. Decorations at the Hôtel Salé and the Hôtel de Beauvais.

Du Cerceau family of architects, including Jean-Baptiste (c.1545–c.1590), who helped design the pont Neuf; Jacques II (c.1550–1614), who worked on the Louvre and the Tuileries; and Jean (c.1590–1649), who designed the Hôtel de Sully and the Hôtel de Bretonvilliers.

Dufy, Raoul (1877–1953) painter, graphic artist and textile designer. Lively colourist, heavily influenced by Matisse. Best known for his exuberant seascapes and beach scenes.

Eiffel, Gustave (1832–1923) engineer, initially known for work on bridges and viaducts: Eiffel Tower constructed for Universal Exhibition of 1889. Collaborated on Bon Marché department store.

Epstein, Sir Jacob (1880–1959) American-born sculptor, active mainly in England. Studied in Paris 1902–5 and mixed with the School of Paris circle. Tomb of Oscar Wilde.

Fantin-Latour, Henri (1836–1904) painter and lithographer, best known for lavish flower pictures.

Foujita, Tsuguharu (or Léonard) (1886–1968) Japanese painter and draughtsman, who settled in Paris in 1913. Links with the School of Paris.

Garnier, Charles (1825–98) architect of the Second Empire, principally known for the Opéra (1862–75).

Gauguin, Paul (1848–1903) painter and graphic artist, a leading figure in the Post-Impressionist and Symbolist movements. His early Impressionist style was superseded by a taste for primitivism that stemmed from his lengthy stays in Tahiti.

Géricault, Théodore (1791–1824) romantic painter, best known for his horse-racing pictures, his portraits of mental patients, and his treatment of macabre subjects.

Gogh, Vincent van (1853–90) Dutch-born painter and draughtsman, working mainly in France. Close links with Gauguin. His emotionally charged pictures, with their vibrant and expressive colouring, influenced most branches of modern art. His career was cut short by mental breakdown and eventual suicide.

Goujon, Jean (*c.*1510–68) architect and sculptor, active in Rouen and Paris. Sculptural decoration at the Louvre. Reliefs at Hôtel Carnavalet.

Gris, Juan (real name José González) (1887–1927) Spanish painter, designer and illustrator, who settled in Paris in 1906. Important figure in Cubist movement, making extensive use of paper collages.

Guimard, Hector (1867–1942) architect and designer, a leading exponent of art nouveau. Best known for his varied entrances to the Métro.

Hardouin-Mansart, Jules (1646–1708) architect, the grand-nephew of François Mansart. Appointed Royal Architect 1675. Extensions at Versailles. Invalides church (1680–91). Place Vendôme (1685).

Haussmann, Baron Georges-Eugène (1809–91) lawyer and civil servant, appointed Prefect of the Seine under Napoleon III. Responsible for the radical redevelopment of the city.

Houdon, Jean-Antoine (1741–1828) sculptor, renowned especially for his portrait busts (e.g. 'Voltaire', Comédie Française). Narrowly escaped imprisonment during the Revolution but regained popularity after the rise of Napoleon.

Ingres, Jean-Auguste-Dominique (1780–1867) painter and draughtsman, working in a graceful, neoclassical style. Excelled at portraiture and history painting. Exotic harem pictures. Delacroix's chief rival in the Salon.

La Tour, Georges de (1593–1652) painter from Lorraine, whose reputation has blossomed in the twentieth century after long neglect. Celebrated for his majestic nocturnal scenes, usually on religious themes.

Le Brun, Charles (1619–90) painter, draughtsman and decorative artist. Director of Académie and Gobelins Factory, 1663. Important decorative schemes at Louvre (Galerie d'Apollon) and at Versailles (Galerie des Glaces).

Léger, Fernand (1881–1955) painter, decorative artist and designer. Noted for his individual brand of Cubism, with its emphasis on tubular forms and modern machinery.

Le Lorrain, Robert (1666–1743) sculptor, famous for his high relief of the *Horses of Apollo* at the stables of the Hôtel de Rohan.

Le Nôtre, André (1613–1700) landscape gardener, specialising in grandiose formal designs. Royal gardener, 1637. Work at Versailles, Saint-Cloud and Tuileries.

Le Vau, Louis (1612–70) major baroque architect. Converted Versailles from a hunting lodge into a royal palace. Notable work at the Louvre, Hôtel Lambert (1640–4) and Hôtel de Fontenay (1656).

Manet, Edouard (1832–83) painter and graphic artist. Came to prominence at the Salon des Refusés with his scandalous *Déjeuner sur l'herbe* (Musée d'Orsay). His scenes of modern Parisian life exerted a powerful influence on the younger artists of the Impressionist group.

Mansart, François (1598–1666) classical architect. Hôtel de la Vrillière provided model for classical Parisian town-house. Remodelled Hôtel Carnavalet (1655). Sainte-Marie de la Visitation (1632–4).

Matisse, Henri (1869–1954) painter, sculptor, draughtsman and designer. Leader of the Fauvist group. His glowing, sensual colours reflected his love of the Riviera, where he spent much of his career.

Mazarin, Cardinal Jules (1602–61) statesman and patron. Art collection swelled after sale of Charles I of England's pictures, 1648. Founded Hôpital de la Salpêtrière (1656) and the Collège des Quatre Nations (1661).

Miró, Joan (1893–1983) Spanish painter and decorative artist, largely resident in Paris between 1919–40. Important member of the Surrealist movement. Huge ceramic murals at Unesco Building.

Mitterand, François (President 1981–) statesman and patron. Commissioned important series of buildings for Bicentenary celebrations, including the Louvre Pyramid, the Géode, the Opéra de la Bastille.

Modigliani, Amedeo (1884–1920) Italian painter and sculptor, working in the School of Paris circle. Celebrated for the sensual, elongated nude studies of his mistress, Jeanne Hébuterne.

Monet, Claude Oscar (1840–1926) foremost Impressionist painter. His 'Impression:Sunrise' gave the movement its name. Clung rigidly to the principle of open-air painting, often producing series of pictures on the same subject, painted under different light conditions. In later life, concentrated on the portrayal of his garden at Giverny and left a series of paintings of it to the nation, which are displayed in the Orangerie.

Montreuil (or Montereau), Pierre de (*d.*1267) master mason. Work at the cathedrals of Notre-Dame and Saint-Denis is ascribed to him.

Moreau, Gustave (1826–98) leading Symbolist painter, with a taste for depicting mysterious and exotic mythologies. The artist's private means freed him from any pressure to sell his paintings and the bulk of his work is preserved at the Musée Moreau.

Nanteuil, Robert (*c*.1623–78) draughtsman and engraver, almost exclusively of portraits. Appointed royal draughtsman in 1658. Executed fine pastel portraits of Louis XIV and his circle.

Picasso, Pablo (1881–1973) Spanish painter, draughtsman and designer, the most influential artist of the twentieth century. Leading figure in the School of Paris. 'Blue Period'. 1901–4. 'Rose Period' 1905–8. Co-founder of the Cubist movement. Close links with the Surrealists. Lived in Paris during the Occupation, later moving to the South of France.

Pigalle, Jean-Baptiste (1714–85) versatile sculptor, with work ranging from portraits to tomb sculpture. His nude figure of Voltaire (Institut de France) is especially notable.

Pilon, Germain (1527–90) sculptor of tomb effigies, medals and portrait busts. Influenced by the School of Fontainebleau. Remarkable tomb sculpture at Saint-Denis.

Poussin, Nicolas (1593/4–1665) enormously influential painter, draughtsman and decorative artist. Mainstay of the French classical tradition. Painted mythologies, landscapes and religious pictures.

Pradier, Jean Jacques (or James) (1790–1852) Swiss neoclassical sculptor, active in France. Carved symbolic Victory figures for Napoleon's tomb (Les Invalides).

Puvis de Chavannes, Pierre (1824–98) symbolist painter and decorative artist. Murals in the Panthéon, the Sorbonne and the Hôtel de Ville.

Renoir, Pierre-Auguste (1841–1919) leading Impressionist painter, present at their first three exhibitions. Painted fleshy nudes, landscapes and joyous scenes of modern life. Continued to work, even when crippled by rheumatism in old age.

Richelieu, Armand Jean de Plessis, Cardinal/Duc de (1585–1642) statesman, collector and patron. Amassed fine library and art collection, the latter eventually passing to Louis XIV. Patron of Poussin. Rebuilt Sainte-Ursule de la Sorbonne and buried there.

Rigaud, Hyacinthe (1659–1743) successful court painter, best known for his imposing state portrait of Louis XIV (Louvre).

Rodin, Auguste (1840–1917) greatest sculptor of his period. Museum housed in Hôtel Biron. Controversial statue of Balzac (blvd. Raspail).

Rouault, Georges (1871–1958) painter, graphic artist and designer of stained glass and tapestries. Moreau was his teacher and Rouault became the first curator of the Musée Moreau.

Rousseau, Henri Julien 'Le Douanier' (1844–1910) celebrated naïve painter. Nickname derived from his job with the Paris Customs Office. Famed for his exotic jungle scenes, which were actually inspired by local botanical gardens. Fêted by the Surrealists.

Rude, François (1784–1855) romantic sculptor, a fervent supporter of Napoleon. Justly renowned for the heroic reliefs on the Arc de Triomphe.

Schöffer, Nicolas (b.1912) Hungarian abstract sculptor, resident in Paris after 1937.

Seurat, Georges (1859–91) painter and draughtsman, the founder of the Neo-Impressionist movement. Participated at the last Impressionist exhibition and at the Salon des Indépendants.

Soufflot, Jacques-Germain (1713–80) neoclassical architect. Celebrated for the Panthéon, the striking result of his studies in Italy. École de Droit (designed 1763). Treasury and sacristy at Notre-Dame (1756).

Soutine, Chaim (1893–1943) Lithuanian painter who settled in France in 1913. Prominent member of the School of Paris. Noted for his intensely emotional portraits.

Toulouse-Lautrec, Henri Marie Raymond de (1864–1901) painter and graphic artist, famed for his scenes of music-halls, cafés and Parisian low-life. His work helped to establish the poster as an art form.

Utrillo, Maurice (1883–1955) self-taught painter. Renowned for his atmospheric street scenes of Montmartre.

Viollet-le-Duc, Eugène-Emmanuel (1814–79) architect and theorist, instigator of the nineteenth-century Gothic revival. Restorer of many medieval buildings, including Sainte Chapelle, Saint-Denis, etc.

Vlaminck, Maurice de (1876–1958) prominent Fauvist painter, heavily influenced by Van Gogh. Shared a studio with Derain. Also a champion cyclist, a talented violinist and a passionate collector of African art.

Watteau, Jean-Antoine (1684–1721) painter and draughtsman, the most important French artist of his period. Specialised in 'fêtes galantes' – lyrical scenes of costumed figures disporting themselves in romantic, pastoral settings.

Whistler, James Abbot McNeill (1834–1903) American painter and graphic artist, active mainly in England. Trained in Paris. Early work influenced by Courbet. Links with the Impressionists.

OPENING TIMES

Most public buildings and churches are open daily, but the latter are liable to be closed to visitors, without notice, during services, and all public buildings are likely to be closed on public holidays. Some of the principal churches are listed below. All hours of opening, including some of those given in the following list, are periodically liable to alteration (winter hours, too, often differ from summer), and it is always advisable to check before planning a visit.

Arc de Triomphe, place Charles-de-Gaulle Étoile: daily 10.00–4.30.

Archives Nationales, Hotel de Soubise, rue des Francs-Bourgeois: daily except Tuesday 2.00–5.00 (joint ticket with the Hôtel de Rohan).

Bibliothèque de l'Arsénal, rue de Sully: Monday to Friday 10.00–5.00.

Bibliotheque Nationale, rue de Richelieu: daily except Sunday 1.00–5.00.

Cathedrals and churches
   Notre-Dame: Archaeological Crypt, place du Parvis Notre-Dame: April to September 10.00–6.00; October to March 10.00–5.00. Towers, rue du Cloitre Notre-Dame: 10.00–5.30.
   Sacré-Coeur, place du Parvis du Sacré-Coeur: daily 6.00 a.m.–11.00 p.m.
   Saint-Denis, place de l'Hôtel de Ville, St Denis: daily 10.00–4.00 or 6.00.
   Sainte Chapelle, boulevard du Palais: daily 10.00–5.00 or 6.00.
Conciergerie, quai de l'Horloge: 10.00–5.00 or 6.00.

Eiffel Tower, Champ de Mars: lifts daily 10.00 a.m.–11.00 p.m.; stairs 10.00–6.00.

Gobelins, avenue des Gobelins: guided tours Tuesday to Thursday at 2.15.

Hôtel de Rohan, rue Vieille du Temple: daily except Tuesday 2.00–5.00 (joint ticket with the Archives Nationales).

Hôtel de Sens, rue du Figuier: Tuesday to Saturday 1.30–8.00.

Hôtel de Sully, rue Saint-Antoine: 10.00–12.30, 2.00–6.00; guided tours Wednesday, Saturday and Sunday afternoons.

Institut du Monde Arabe, quai Saint-Bernard: daily except Monday 1.00–8.00.

Invalides, Esplanade des Invalides: daily 10.00–6.00.

Jardin des Plantes, rue Cuvier: daily except Tuesday 9.00–5.00 or 6.00 (Zoological Gardens open daily).

Museums and galleries
   de l'Armée (see Invalides).
   Balzac, rue Raynouard: daily except Monday 10.00–5.40.
   Carnavalet, rue de Sévigné: daily except Monday 10.00–5.40.
   Cernuschi, avenue Velasquez: daily except Monday 10.00–5.40.
   de la Chasse, rue des Archives: daily except Tuesday 10.00–12.30, 1.30–5.30.
   Cluny, pl Paul-Painlevé: daily except Tuesday 9.45–12.30, 2.00–5.15.
   Guimet, place d'Iéna: daily except Tuesday 9.45–12.00, 1.30–5.15.
   Grévin, boulevard de Montmartre: Monday to Saturday 1.00–7.00; Sunday 1.00–6.00.
   Hugo, Victor, places des Vosges: daily except Monday 10.00–5.40.
   Louvre, Palais du Louvre: daily except Tuesday 9.45–5.00 or 6.00.
   Marmottan, rue Louis-Boilly: daily except Monday 10.00–5.30.

Nationale des Arts et Traditions Populaires, avenue du Mahatma-Ghandi: daily except Tuesday 10.00–5.15.
Picasso, rue de Thorigny: Thursday to Monday 9.15–5.15; Wednesday 9.15 a.m.–10.00 p.m.
Pompidou Centre, rue Saint-Martin: Monday, Wednesday, Thursday and Friday 12.00–10.00; Saturday and Sunday 10.00–10.00.
Nissim de Camondo, rue de Monceau: daily except Monday and Tuesday 10.00–12.00, 2.00–5.00.
Orangerie, place de la Concorde: daily except Tuesday 9.45–5.15.
d'Orsay, rue de Bellechasse: Tuesday, Wednesday, Friday and Saturday 10.30–6.00; Sunday 9.00–6.00; Thursday 10.30–9.45.
de la Poste, boulevard Vaugirard: daily except Sunday 10.00–5.00.
Rodin, rue de Varenne: daily except Tuesday 10.00–5.00.

Palais de Luxembourg, rue de Vaugirard: guided tours Sunday 9.30–11.00, 2.00–4.00.
Palais de Tokyo, avenue du Président Wilson: daily 10.00–5.00.

Tour Montparnasse, avenue du Maine: April to September daily 9.30–11.00; October to March daily 10.00–10.00.

Versailles: Château daily except Monday 9.45–5.30; Grand Trianon daily except Monday 9.45–12.00, 2.00–5.30; Petit Trianon daily except Monday 2.00–5.30.

Glossary of Terms

························

Ambulatory Continuation of the aisles around the east end of a church.

Archivolts Series of mouldings on the face of an arch.

Art Nouveau Style of painting and design which flourished between 1890–1914. Characterized by flowing, sinuous lines and plant-like forms.

Belle Époque Loose term describing the graceful style of living enjoyed from the 1890s until World War I.

Commune Revolutionary uprising in Paris in 1871, following defeat in the Franco-Prussian War. The aim was to gain greater independence from the national government, but the rebellion was bloodily suppressed.

Cubism Art movement pioneered by Braque and Picasso in the first decade of the twentieth century. The Cubists abandoned the traditional aim of imitating nature through perspective and modelling, depicting it instead with flat, planar surfaces.

Dormer window Small, gabled window projecting from a sloping roof.

Edict of Nantes Decree of Henri IV, 1598, allowing Huguenots freedom of worship. The Revocation of the Edict in 1685 was followed by the mass-emigration of this Protestant group.

Encyclopédiste In the wake of Diderot's *Encyclopédie* (completed 1772), an upholder of rational beliefs. Implied a political and anti-clerical stance. Seen as an important factor in the growth of Revolutionary feeling.

Existentialism Philosophy which denies objective universal ideals, emphasising the need for the individual to create personal values based on action and experience. In France, the movement was popularised by Jean-Paul Sartre.

Fauvism Style of painting developed in the first decade of the twentieth century. The term 'fauve' ('wild beast') was used by a critic to describe the group's use of pure, brilliant colours and the vitality of their decorative effects. Their leader was Matisse.

Flying Buttress Arch or half-arch set against an outer wall to strengthen it against the thrust of a vault.

Fontainebleau, School of Term applied to the elegant style of painting and decoration developed at the French court during the sixteenth century.

Fronde Civil disturbances in 1648–53, during the minority of Louis XIV. Partly a revolt against Mazarin and partly a factional dispute between the nobility. Named after the slings used by the Paris mob.

Futurism Short-lived artistic movement, founded in 1909 by the poet Marinetti. It sought to break with the past by celebrating the glories of machinery and the dynamism of the modern age.

Gothic Style of European art and architecture prevalent from the late twelfth to the early sixteenth century. Characterized by pointed arches, flying buttresses and elaborate tracery.

Imagism Anti-Romantic school of poetry founded by Ezra Pound.

Impressionism Art movement originating in France in the 1860s. The aim was to capture the immediacy of visual impressions, rather than to provide a single, definitive record of a place or object. There were eight official Impressionist exhibitions (1874–86).

Merovingians Dynasty descended from Merovius which ruled over the Franks from the fifth century until 751.

Paris, School of Loose term applied to the international community of artists which gathered in Paris in the early years of the twentieth century. The term also embraces the styles (e.g. Fauvism, Cubism) which developed there.

Pediment Triangular gable above a doorway or window.

Pendant Ornament of stone or wood hanging from a roof.

Philosophes General term for the eighteenth-century men of letters and science who believed in the supremacy of reason. Provided the intellectual momentum for the French Revolution.

Pier Heavy masonry support, thicker than a column.

Pléiade Group of sixteenth-century French poets, led by Ronsard, who echoed the style of the ancient Greeks and Romans.

Portal Doorway or arch above an entrance.

Post-Impressionism Term coined by Roger Fry to describe the differing reactions to Impressionism in the period *c.*1880–*c.*1905. Refers to artists such as Gauguin, Van Gogh, Cézanne and Seurat, each of whom rebelled against the naturalistic aims of the Impressionists, either by using formal simplifications or by adding a spiritual dimension to their work.

Putti (sing. putto) Painting or carved figures of naked, angelic children.

Renaissance European intellectual movement, affecting all branches of the arts. The term means 'rebirth', alluding to the rediscovery of antique learning and culture. The movement originated in Italy in *c.*1400. It reached France in the following century, leaving its mark on the School of Fontainebleau.

Romanesque European style of painting and architecture, at its peak in the eleventh and twelfth centuries. Typified in buildings by round arches and in painting by linear, stylized forms.

Rood screen Screen between choir and nave bearing a rood or cross.

Sacristy Area in church where the sacred utensils and vestments are kept.

Salon Periodic gathering of a literary or social coterie.

Salon, the Official art exhibition held by members of the Académie. Name derived from its original venue, the Salon d'Apollon in the Louvre. By the nineteenth century, the Salon had acquired the reputation of being a bastion of conservatism.

Salon des Indépendants Exhibition held annually by the Société des Artistes Indépendants from 1884 until the outbreak of World War I. The group had no selection committee and their exhibitions thus became a showcase for progressive talents.

Salon des Refusés Exhibition held in 1863 by artists who had been rejected by the official salon. Exhibitors included Manet, Cézanne and Whistler.

Scholasticism Doctrines of the medieval teachers of theology and philosophy.

Second Empire Restoration of the French Empire during the reign of Napoleon III (1852–70), the nephew of Napoleon Bonaparte.

Stoup A holy-water vessel.

Structuralism Analytical linguistic theory developed in France in the 1960s.

Surrealism Literary and artistic movement stemming from André Breton's *Manifesto* (1924). The Surrealists explored the realms of dreams, the unconscious and the irrational.

Tracery Decorative stone framework of a gothic window.

Triforium Arcaded wall passage above the nave.

Trompe-l'oeil In painting, an illusionistic effect which gives a three-dimensional appearance to a flat image.

Tympanum Semi-circular area between the lintel of a doorway and the arch above it.

Further Reading

....

Baldick, Robert, ed., *Pages from the Goncourt Journal*, London 1962

Balzac, Honoré de, *Lost Illusions*, Paris, 1837–43

Blunt, Anthony, *Art and Architecture in France 1500 to 1700*, London, 1953

Flaubert, Gustave, *A Sentimental Education*, Paris, 1869

Hemingway, Ernest, *A Moveable Feast*, London, 1964

Hibbert, Christopher, *The French Revolution*, London, 1981

Hillairet, Jacques, *Dictionnaire Historique des Rues de Paris*, Paris, 1963

Littlewood, Ian, *Paris: A Literary Companion*, London, 1987

Lucie-Smith, Edward, *A Concise History of French Painting*, London, 1971

Miller, Henry, *Tropic of Cancer*, Paris, 1934

Orwell, George, *Down and Out in Paris and London*, London, 1933

Rhys, Jean, *Quartet*, London, 1928

Russell, John, *Paris*, London, 1960

Sévigné, Madame de, *Selected Letters*, Harmondsworth, 1982

Zola, Emile, *L'Assommoir*, Paris, 1877
Nana, Paris, 1880

Index

·····························

References to illustrations appear in italics, after the text references.